Strategies for Test-Taking Success:

Christy M. Newman

HEINLE
CENGAGE Learning™

Australia • Brazil • Japan • Korea • Mexico • Singapore • Spain • United Kingdom • United States

Strategies for Test-Taking Success: Writing
Christy M. Newman

Publisher: Phyllis Dobbins

Director of Product Development:
Anita Raducanu

Director, ELL Training and Development:
Evelyn Nelson

Director of Product Marketing: Amy Mabley

Product Marketing Manager: Laura Needham

Sr. Field Marketing Manager: Robert Walters

Associate Development Editor: John Hicks

Editorial Assistant: Lindsey Musen

Production Editor: Chrystie Hopkins

Manufacturing Manager: Marcia Locke

Development Editor: Weston Editorial

Design and Production Services:
Pre-Press Company, Inc.

Cover Designer: Studio Montage

Printer: Banta Book Group

© 2006 Heinle, Cengage Learning

For permission to use material from this text or product,
submit all requests online at **cengage.com/permissions**
Further permissions questions can be emailed to
permissionrequest@cengage.com

Library of Congress Control Number: 2005911264

ISBN-10: 1-4130-0926-3
ISBN-13: 978-1-4130-0926-2

ISE ISBN-10: 1-4130-1994-3
ISE ISBN-13: 978-1-4130-1994-0

Heinle
25 Thomson Place
Boston, MA 02210
USA

Cengage Learning is a leading provider of customized learning solutions with office locations around the globe, including Singapore, the United Kingdom, Australia, Mexico, Brazil, and Japan. Locate your local office at:
international.cengage.com/region

Cengage Learning products are represented in Canada by Nelson Education, Ltd.

Visit Heinle online at **elt.heinle.com**
Visit our corporate website at **cengage.com**

Printed in the United States of America
4 5 6 7 11 10 09 08

Table of Contents

Acknowledgments

I wish to thank Sophia Wisener of R. S. Wise Editing Services for meeting the challenge with creativity and aplomb, and John Hicks for his keen editorial eye.

Thanks also to Phyllis Dobbins and Anita Raducanu for their friendship and encouragement during the creation of *Strategies for Test-Taking Success,* and to the following people at Thomson ELT: Evelyn Nelson, Chrystie Hopkins, Bridget McLaughlin, and Lindsey Musen.

Jonathan, Corey, and Tom: You are the point of it all.

I dedicate this series to Anna Newman, who learned English as a second language in New York City's public schools.

Christy M. Newman

Reviewers

Maryanne Danielle Bragaw
  Austin Independent School District
  Bedichek Middle School
  Austin, TX

Heather Cooper
  Huntington Beach Union High School
    District
  Marina High School
  Huntington Beach, CA

Pompeya Gettler
  Clark County School District
  K. O. Knudson Middle School
  Las Vegas, NV

Lori Langer de Ramirez
  Herricks Union Free School District
  New Hyde Park, NY

Gina McNeil
  Orange County Public Schools
  West Orange High School
  West Orange, NJ

Sandy Wagner
  Ft. Lauderdale High School
  Broward County Public Schools
  Fort Lauderdale, FL

Peggy Wheeler
  Anne Arundel County Public Schools
  Annapolis High School
  Annapolis, MD

About This Book

STRATEGIES FOR TEST-TAKING SUCCESS is a test preparation series designed to help *all* students develop effective test-taking skills and strategies. The series uses clear, easy-to-understand language and examples, with illustrations and activities. It provides support for foundation skills. It also teaches and practices advanced skills and concepts in an easy, accessible way. The series incorporates scientifically based research in the areas of reading, math, and writing.

Features

- The **instructional chapters** focus on major skills and standards concepts tested in most standardized state tests. Each chapter is divided into short lessons, called **Strategies**. Each Strategy focuses on a discrete skill or concept. The techniques rely on proven test-taking strategies.

- **Clear, simple language** and **illustrations** support higher-order thinking skills.

- The **Pretest** helps evaluate current skills. Areas-of-need are recorded on a **Skills Chart**.

- **Keys To Understanding** highlight key words, questions, and/or special test-taking pointers to learn.

- **Tips** offer practical aids and hints.

- **Practice Questions** review skills and concepts taught in the lesson. They progress from controlled to productive and open-ended questions.

- The **Review Tests** and two **Cumulative Practice Tests** simulate the format, length, and language of authentic standardized tests. Questions ask about newly taught material and recycle what was taught earlier.

- The **Answer Key** thoroughly explains both correct and incorrect answer choices.

- The reproducible **Answer Grid** is used to practice filling in "bubble sheets" for standardized tests.

- English and Spanish **Glossaries** define key writing terms.

- ExamView Pro® software allows for test item customization, re-testing, and computer-delivered practice.

How to Use This Book

Students can use this book to study and review for standardized state tests. This book helps students understand what a standardized test is like. They learn the best ways to take standardized tests and practice taking them.

Teachers can use this book as a "reteach and reassess" tool to target specific standards-based skills and concepts where additional practice is needed. It can also be used for whole-class instruction or as an individual tutorial.

References

California Department of Education. 1996. *Practical Ideas for Teaching Writing as a Process at the Elementary School and Middle School Levels*. Edited by C.B. Olson. Sacramento: California Department of Education.

Calkins, L. 1994. *The Art of Teaching Writing*. Portsmouth, NH: Heinemann.

Graham, S., Harris, K. R., MacArthur, C. A., & Schwartz, S. 1991. "Writing and writing instruction for students with learning disabilities: Review of a research program." *Learning Disability Quarterly,* 14(2), 89-114.

Schumaker, J. B., & Sheldon, J. (1985). *The sentence writing strategy*. Lawrence, KS: The University of Kansas.

Spandel, V. 1998. *Seeing with New Eyes: A Guidebook on Teaching and Assessing Beginning Writers* (Fourth edition). Portland, OR: Northwest Regional Educational Laboratory.

Supon, V. 2004. "Implementing Strategies to Assist Test-Anxious Students" *Journal of Instructional Psychology,* Vol. 31, 2004

Chapter 1 Introduction

Writing Pretest

The Writing Pretest tells you two important things:

- **What you know.** The Writing Pretest shows you the writing skills you have now. Review those skills or start to learn and practice new ones.

- **What you need to learn.** The Writing Pretest shows you the writing skills you need to learn and practice.

Directions: The Writing Pretest has 24 questions.

1. Read each question carefully.

2. Look at any pictures, diagrams, or extra information.

3. Answer all the questions. Pick only one answer for each question.

4. Mark your answers on the Answer Grid.

EXAMPLE:
17. (A) (B) ● (D)

ANSWER GRID

1. (A) (B) (C) (D)	9. (A) (B) (C) (D)	17. (A) (B) (C) (D)
2. (A) (B) (C) (D)	10. (A) (B) (C) (D)	18. (A) (B) (C) (D)
3. (A) (B) (C) (D)	11. (A) (B) (C) (D)	19. (A) (B) (C) (D)
4. (A) (B) (C) (D)	12. (A) (B) (C) (D)	20. (A) (B) (C) (D)
5. (A) (B) (C) (D)	13. (A) (B) (C) (D)	21. (A) (B) (C) (D)
6. (A) (B) (C) (D)	14. (A) (B) (C) (D)	22. (A) (B) (C) (D)
7. (A) (B) (C) (D)	15. (A) (B) (C) (D)	23. (A) (B) (C) (D)
8. (A) (B) (C) (D)	16. (A) (B) (C) (D)	24. (A) (B) (C) (D)

Writing Pretest

Mark your answers on the Answer Grid.

Read this story. Answer Questions 1 through 6.

(1) The Sun and the North Wind were arguing.

(2) "Every living thing needs the power of my light and heat. (3) That's why I am far more powerful than you were," said the Sun.

(4) "Nonsense," said the North Wind. (5) "You can't beat me. (6) I can blow forests down and start storms that last 100 years! (7) I can make humans shake with fear!"

(8) "Then I challenge you to a contest," said the Sun. (9) "Look down at that traveler. (10) I think he is going to Athens. (11) Let us see who can get his coat off first."

(12) The North Wind went first. (13) He blew a fierce wind at the man. (14) "I'll show that Sun who is top banana around here," the North Wind said to himself. (15) But the harder he blew, the tighter he clutched his coat around him.

(16) First, he sent down gentle sunbeams, and the traveler unbuttoned his coat. (17) Next, the Sun slowly turned on his warmth. (18) Soon the man took off his coat and went on his way.

—adapted from *Aesop's Fables*

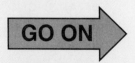

1 **This story is an example of —**

A a persuasive essay

B the Writing Process

C a narrative

D an expository essay

2 **Which sentence does NOT belong in this story?**

A Sentence 6

B Sentence 8

C Sentence 10

D Sentence 12

3 **Which sentence has tone and language that don't fit the reading?**

A Sentence 12

B Sentence 13

C Sentence 14

D Sentence 15

4 **You can improve the meaning of sentence 15 by changing the second *he* to —**

A the traveler

B the North Wind

C them

D him

5 **What sentence belongs *before* sentence 16?**

A The traveler's coat did not come off.

B The North Wind gave up.

C It got hotter and hotter.

D Then the Sun took his turn.

6 **Which answer best states the lesson, or moral, of the story?**

A Be happy with what you have.

B Persuasion works better than force.

C You can't teach an old dog new tricks.

D Necessity is the mother of invention.

short

grandmother

nice to everyone

her neighborhood is quiet

pretty, dark, curly hair

7 Look at Maria's Writing Plan. Which detail does not belong?

A   short

B   nice to everyone

C   her neighborhood is quiet

D   pretty, dark, curly hair

8 What kind of paper is Maria going to write?

A   a paper that explains where her grandmother lives

B   a paper that tells about her grandmother's hairstyle

C   a paper that lists directions

D   a paper that describes her favorite relative

9 How should the underlined part of this sentence be rewritten to create parallel structure?

Instant messaging is a <u>quick, easy, and enjoyably fun</u> way to contact friends.

A   more fast, more easy, and enjoyable

B   quickly, easier, and enjoyable

C   quick, easy, and most fun

D   quick, easy, and enjoyable

Strategies for Test-Taking Success: Writing © Heinle, Cengage Learning. Photocopying this page is prohibited by law.

For questions 10 through 13, choose the word or phrase that best completes the sentence.

10 Please get some stamps when you go _____ the post office.

   A to

   B too

   C two

   D though

11 You can get excellent directions online, _____ you must use a good search engine.

   A if

   B but

   C yet

   D which

12 Midas wanted to be the _____ king in the world.

   A richer

   B richest

   C more richer

   D most richest

13 Look at the underlined word. Which word makes the sentence correct?

> She <u>are</u> going to the movies with her friends.

   A was

   B were

   C have been

   D Correct as is.

14 Look at the underlined words. Which transition is better?

> There were no electric lights in most homes in 1900. <u>In addition,</u> most homes had kerosene or gas lamps.

A Also

B First

C Instead

D Much later

15 Which word or words should go in the blank?

> Roberto and Federico are twins. Paco is _____ little brother.

A their

B there

C they're

D they are

16 Which word should go in the blank?

> Linda washed the dishes. Then she put _____ away.

A it

B they

C her

D them

17 In which sentence is all the capitalization correct?

A Thanksgiving Day is on the last thursday in november.

B Thanksgiving Day is on the last Thursday in November.

C Thanksgiving day is on the last thursday in November.

D Thanksgiving Day is on the Last Thursday in november.

18 In which sentence is all the punctuation correct?

A Dads pie recipe uses butter apples flour and sugar.

B Dads pie recipe use's butter, apple's, flour, and sugar.

C Dad's pie recipe uses butter, apples, flour, and sugar.

D Dads pie recipe uses butter, apples, flour, and sugar?

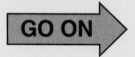
GO ON

Strategies for Test-Taking Success: Writing © Heinle, Cengage Learning. Photocopying this page is prohibited by law.

Read this sentence.

> Wednesday, April 23 is the last day to buy tickets for the Spring Dance no tickets will be sold at the door.

19 **What is the best way to write the information in the box?**

  A Wednesday, April 23 is the last day to buy tickets for the Spring Dance, no tickets will be sold at the door.

  B Wednesday April 23 is the last day to buy tickets for the Spring Dance; No tickets will be sold at the door.

  C Wednesday, April 23, is the last day to buy tickets for the Spring Dance. No tickets will be sold at the door.

  D Make no change.

---

20 **Which answer has the best word choice?**

  A School concerts are very popular. When there isn't enough room in the auditorium for everyone, we hold the event in the gym.

  B Sometimes a lot of people come to popular concerts. They can't fit in the auditorium. Then we have a gym event instead.

  C Too many people go to musical exhibitions, so the audience has to sit in the gym.

  D When there are too many people in the auditorium, go to the gym to hear a concert.

Read this paragraph.

> (1) Hats are too much trouble. (2) They are unattractive. (3) They get lost. (4) Kids put them down and forget where. (5) When hats fall on the floor, it gets dirty and wet. (6) Hats just aren't cool.

21 Which sentence should be added to the *beginning* of the paragraph?

 A   I never wear a hat.

 B   Straw hats are itchy, and woolen hats are hot.

 C   There are many reasons why kids don't like to wear hats.

 D   A graduation cap is a *mortarboard*.

22 Which sentence adds interesting detail to the paragraph?

 A   I never wear a hat.

 B   Straw hats are itchy, and woolen hats are hot.

 C   There are many reasons kids don't like to wear hats.

 D   A graduation cap is a *mortarboard*.

23 What change should be made in sentence 5?

 A   Delete *When*.

 B   Change *hats fall* to *hats fell*.

 C   Change *it gets* to *they get*.

 D   Make no change.

24 Which transition word or phrase should be added to the beginning of sentence 6?

 A   First of all,

 B   However,

 C   For example,

 D   Most of all,

STOP. THIS IS THE END OF THE WRITING PRETEST.   STOP

Answer Key to the Writing Pretest

1. ✓ Check *correct* answers. ⬭ Circle *incorrect* answers.

1. C	7. C	13. A	19. C
2. C	8. D	14. C	20. A
3. C	9. D	15. A	21. C
4. A	10. A	16. D	22. B
5. D	11. B	17. B	23. C
6. B	12. B	18. C	24. D

2. Circle the numbers of the incorrect answers from part 1 on the **Skills Chart**.

SKILLS CHART

Circle Incorrect Answers	Skill Area	Chapters to Study
4, 12, 13, 16, 23	Grammar	Chapter 2 (page 19)
10, 15, 17, 18	Spelling and Mechanics	Chapter 3 (page 45)
9, 11, 19, 20	Sentences	Chapter 4 (page 69)
2, 3, 5, 14, 21, 22	Paragraphs	Chapter 5 (page 91)
1, 6, 7, 8, 24	Essays	Chapter 6 (page 115)

3. Circle the chapters you need to study. (*Hint:* You probably need to work on areas with two or more incorrect answers.)

Strategize for the Test

1. **Before you study:** Think about the big picture. Think about all the steps on the way to test-taking success. Study and practice your writing skills *over time*. Don't wait until the last minute to practice writing. Plan to make writing a *habit*.

2. **Assess your skills:** Look at the Skills Chart on page 9. Are most of your answers correct? Maybe you need to review one chapter. Then, 15–20 minutes a day may be enough study time. Or, you may need to study more chapters. Then an hour or more a day may be enough time.

3. **Make your plan:** Count your study days between today and the test. Don't count the days when you are very busy.

Sun	Mon	Tue	Wed	Thu	Fri	Sat
	1 *Today:* *Make a* *plan*	2 *5:00–6* *Study* *time*	3 *5:00–6* *Study* *time*	4 *5:00–6* *Study* *time*	5 *5:00–6* *Study* *time*	6 *5:00–6* *Study* *time*
7	8 *5:00–6* *Study* *time*	9 *5:00–6* *Study* *time*	10 *Study for* *science* *test*	11 *5:00–6* *Study* *time*	12 *5:00–6* *Study* *time*	13 *5:00–6* *Study* *time*
14	15 *5:00–6* *Study* *time*	16 *5:00–6* *Study* *time*	17 *5:00–6* *Study* *time*	18 *5:00–6* *Study* *time*	19 *Birthday* *party* *for Dad*	20 *5:00–6* *Study* *time*
21	22 *5:00–6* *Study* *time*	23 *5:00–6* *Study* *time*	24 *5:00–6* *Study* *time*	25 *5:00–6* *Study* *time*	26 *5:00–6* *Study* *time*	27 *School* *play*
28	29 *5:00–6* *Study* *time*	30 *Relax*	31 *TEST*			

4. **Decide how long to study each day:** Write the time you need to study on a calendar or in a notebook. Check off each day when you finish your work.

5. **Strategize for success:** Keep to your plan. That way you will be prepared. You won't get stressed out. You won't have to cram (study a lot just before the test). Instead, you can relax and get a good night's sleep. You will be ready on the day of the test.

Learn about Question Types and General Test-Taking Strategies

It is helpful to know what is on the writing test. This section tells about three kinds of questions. It gives you strategies for answering the questions, too.

Types of Test Questions

1. **Multiple Choice:** Every test has many multiple-choice questions. (All questions on the Writing Pretest are multiple choice.)

   A multiple-choice question has two parts: (1) a **stem** or **question** and (2) the **answer choices**. There are usually four answer choices. You pick *one*.

You can improve the meaning of sentence 15 by changing the second *he* to—

> The **stem** asks the *question.*

(15) But the harder he blew, the tighter he clutched his coat around him.

    A the traveler

    B the North Wind

    C them

    D him

> The **answer choices** are *A, B, C,* or *D.*

2. **Short Answer:** Some standardized tests have **short-answer** questions, too. For these, you write an answer. Short answers are one or two sentences to a paragraph long. Sometimes icons (small pictures) let you know that a question is a short-answer question.

Short-answer questions take about five to fifteen minutes to read, think about, and answer.

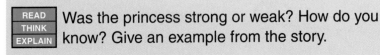 **READ THINK EXPLAIN** Was the princess strong or weak? How do you know? Give an example from the story.

The princess was strong. She showed this by looking the

witch in the eye. The princess didn't let the witch take

the rope either.

3. **Open Response:** Open responses are also called **essays, extended responses,** or **writing tasks.** You write an answer to these questions, too. But these answers are longer than one or two sentences. They are one to five paragraphs. They take more time. You need to use The Writing Process to answer open-response questions. You will learn about the Writing Process in Chapter 6.

The Writing Process

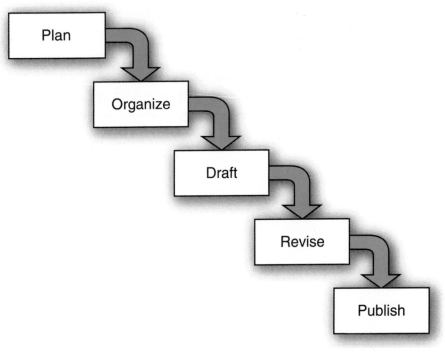

Most questions on state tests are multiple-choice questions. You pick the best answer from four choices. This strategy shows you how to get the right answer.

1. **Read the *statement* or *passage* carefully.** The statement or passage can:

   - be long or short.

   - have a chart or diagram.

   - have a ____(blank)____.

   > Linda washed the dishes. Then she put _____ away.

   - be underlined.

   > There were no electric lights in most homes in 1900. <u>In addition</u>, most homes had kerosene or gas lamps.

2. **Read the *stem* or *question* carefully.**

   > Which detail does not belong in this Writing Plan?

3. **Use *line* or *paragraph numbers*.** Many readings have numbers to help you find information quickly.

   > The meaning of *sentence 15* can be improved by changing the second *he* to _____.

Strategies for Test-Taking Success: Writing © Heinle, Cengage Learning. Photocopying this page is prohibited by law.

4. Answer *every* question. Don't leave any blanks on the answer sheet. Some questions are hard. You may not know an answer. Then it's time to **guess.** Use the process of elimination to make your best guess.

EXAMPLE

Andreas wants to answer Question 15.

Read this paragraph.

(1) Hats are too much trouble. (2) They are unattractive. (3) They get lost. (4) Kids put them down and forget where. (5) When hats fall on the floor, it gets dirty and wet. (6) Hats just aren't cool.

15. **Which sentence below should be added to the *beginning* of the paragraph?**

A I never wear a hat.

B Straw hats are itchy and woolen hats are hot.

C There are many reasons why kids don't like to wear hats.

D A graduation cap is a *mortarboard*.

First, Andreas reads the paragraph carefully. Then he reads the question: Which sentence below should be added to the *beginning* of the paragraph?

Andreas thinks: *Topic sentences are often at the* beginning *of a paragraph. I need to find a topic sentence.*

Next, he looks at the four choices. He still doesn't know the answer.

Then he uses the **process of elimination** to make his best guess. The process of elimination helps him cross out wrong answers.

This is NOT a first-person paragraph. Andreas knows A is wrong.	A̶ I never wear a hat.

Step 2 Use information from the passage only. Cross out answers about anything NOT in the passage.

Andreas sees no information about a graduation cap. This can't be the topic sentence.	D̶ A graduation cap is a *mortarboard*.

Step 3 Make sure an answer is true.

Andreas rereads the paragraph. B and C are both true. Andreas can't cross them out.	B Straw hats are itchy, and woolen hats are hot. C There are many reasons why kids don't like to wear hats.

Step 4 Read the question again. Then make your best guess.

Andreas reads the question again. He thinks: *I'm looking for a topic sentence. This paragraph is about why hats are problems for kids. I think B gives examples. I think C is a topic sentence.* Andreas makes his best guess. He marks C on the answer sheet. Do you agree?

Andreas is correct. C is the best answer.

The Process of Elimination:
How Guessing Helps Your Score

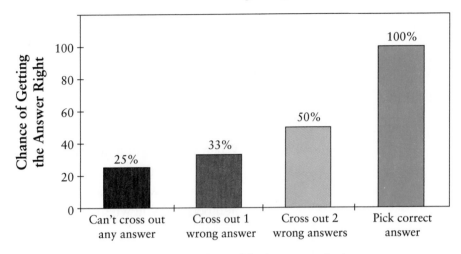

1 question with 4 answer choices

Here's how the **process of elimination** works:

1. You can't cross out ANY answers. The chance of a right guess: 25%.

2. You can cross out **1** wrong answer. The chance of a right guess: 33%.

3. You can cross out **2** wrong answers. The chance of a right guess: 50%!

4. You can cross out **3** wrong answers. You score! That's 100%!

Use these successful strategies as you work in this book and take tests.

1. Read all directions carefully. Don't skim. Ask the test giver questions about the directions.

2. When you answer a question, use the paragraph numbers ("In *paragraph 8,* the author . . .") or line numbers ("According to *lines 17–18,* what does . . .") given in the question. These numbers tell you where the answer is.

3. Answer easy questions first.

4. Don't spend a lot of time on one question. If you're stuck, skip it. You can look at it again after you answer the easy questions. Make sure you have enough time for all questions.

5. Don't change an answer unless you are sure your first choice is wrong.

6. Fill in the answer sheet carefully. Make sure you put your answer in the right place.

Chapter 2

Review Grammar

Strategy 3

Review Parts of Speech

A part of speech is a way to group words that are alike. English has eight parts of speech. The parts of speech in English are nouns, pronouns, verbs, adjectives, adverbs, prepositions, conjunctions, and interjections.

The following sections review the parts of speech and what they mean.

Nouns

A noun names a *person, place, thing,* or *idea*.

EXAMPLE

Person	Place	Thing	Idea
Marty	Florida	Tuesday	equator
mother	state	skateboard	thought
students	school	story	beauty

Underline the nouns in this invitation.

Margarita Soto graduates from
Lincoln School on Saturday, April 3.
Come to a party with family and friends
at the Sotos' house
32 Chavez Avenue
Newtown

You are correct if you underlined *Lincoln School, Saturday, April, party, family, friends, Sotos', house, Chavez Avenue, and Newtown.*

Pronouns

A **pronoun** takes the place of a noun.

EXAMPLE		
Noun	**Pronoun**	**Sentences**
Martin	**he, him, his**	**Martin** is from New York. He is my friend. The kids in my class like him a lot. His family moved here 2 years ago.
mother and I	**we, us, our**	My **mother and I** drive around town. We need to visit my uncle. He usually visits us. Now it's our turn.
Florida	**it, its**	**Florida** is fun to visit. It has beautiful beaches. Its beaches are world famous.
friends	**they, them, their**	My four **friends** are doing homework together. They are in the library. I am going to join them. Their favorite spot to study is on the first floor.

Read this note. Then match the nouns and pronouns that replace them.

Dear Margarita,

Kim and I arrive in Newtown on April 2. We will stay at Bonita's house. We can walk to the party with her. It will be fun.

We are so proud of you!

Sonja Alvarez

__d__ I		a. Bonita
_____ 1. We		b. Margarita
_____ 2. her		c. Kim and Sonja
_____ 3. It		d. Sonja Alvarez
_____ 4. you		e. party

1. c;   2. a;   3. e;   4. b

Verbs

A **verb** tells what a noun or pronoun *is* or *does*. There are *action* and *nonaction* verbs.

Action verbs describe *movement*. **Nonaction** verbs describe *feelings* or *how something is*.

The boy <u>runs</u> in the park.

The parents <u>love</u> their baby.

Lunch <u>is</u> ready.

EXAMPLE

Action Verbs	Nonaction Verbs
run	is
write	feel
listen	need

Look at the words. Cross out the word in each line that is not a verb.

Example: jump   sing   ~~shoe~~

A. say   tell   dad   speak

B. us   go   ask   know

C. play   Tuesday   want   are

A. *dad* is a noun (person); B. *us* is a pronoun;
C. *Tuesday* is a noun (thing)

Adjectives tell about *nouns* or *pronouns*. Adjectives answer: *Which one? What kind? How many?*

> **EXAMPLE**
>
> *Which one?*   the **tall** man
>
> *What kind?*   a **cloudy** sky
>
> *How many?*   **seven** days

Adverbs tell about *verbs* or *adjectives*. They also tell about other adverbs. Adverbs answer the questions: *When? Where? How? How often?*

> **EXAMPLE**
>
> *When?*   sing **now, next week**
>
> *Where?*   sing **there, outside**
>
> *How?*   sing **loudly, confidently**
>
> *How often?*   sing **every day, frequently**

TIP

Many adjectives become adverbs when you add -ly to the end.

slow → slowly

careful → carefully

Underline the adjectives. (*Hint:* There are five adjectives.)

The food at my school is <u>delicious</u>. But there's one problem: I am a big eater and the servings are small. You can get second helpings, but there isn't time to eat them. I am hungry after lunch.

Adjectives: one, big, small, second, hungry.

Underline the adverbs. (*Hint:* There is one adverb in each sentence.)

My friends and I <u>always</u> bring our lunch. On nice days, we meet outside. When it rains, we find seats early before the cafeteria is crowded. We eat quickly and have a lot of time to talk. Sometimes we have time for a game of Frisbee.

Adverbs: outside, early, quickly, Sometimes

Prepositions

Prepositions link a noun or pronoun to another word in a sentence. Prepositions help show direction, place, or time.

Here is a list of common prepositions:

about	behind	in	over
above	below	inside	through
across	between	into	to
after	by	near	under
among	down	of	until
around	during	off	up
at	for	on	with
before	from	outside	without

Many prepositions have opposites. Write the opposites of these prepositions.

on / _off_   over / _____   below / _____   down / _____

without / _____   after / _____   out / _____   from / _____

over-under; below-above; down-up; without-with; after-before; out-in; from-to

Conjunctions

Conjunctions join words or parts of a sentence. They can join sentences, too.

> **EXAMPLE**
>
> and　　but　　so　　because

Check the sentence that needs a conjunction.

———— A.　The soccer team is number one in the state.

———— B.　It won the town finals the state finals, too.

> You are correct if you checked B. The conjunction *and* belongs between *town finals* and the *state finals*.

Interjections

Interjections show surprise or strong feelings. Often they are followed by an exclamation point (!).

> **EXAMPLE**
>
> Wow!　　Ouch!　　Whoopee!

Add an interjection to the sentence that shows surprise or strong feelings.

A.　————　That's a wonderful idea.

B.　————　I like the idea.

> Add an interjection such as *Wow*! to A. The word *wonderful* shows strong feeling.

Practice A: Read the paragraph. Answer the questions.

My Cousin Rosa

(1) My favorite relative is my cousin Rosa. (2) She is like a sister to me. (3) We talk every day. (4) She cheers me up when I'm sad. (5) She always tells me the truth, so I trust her. (6) We do everything together. (7) We look alike, too. (8) Once, we wore the same clothes. (9) People thought that we were twins! (10) I am a lucky girl to have a cousin like Rosa.

Example: In sentence 1, what part of speech is *favorite*? _adjective_

1. In sentence 1, what part of speech is *Rosa*? _____

2. In sentence 3, what part of speech is *talk*? _____

3. In sentence 5, what part of speech is *so*? _____

4. In sentence 6, what part of speech is *We*? _____

5. In sentence 8, what part of speech is *Once*? _____

6. In sentence 10, what part of speech is *lucky*? _____

Practice B: Write three sentences in your notebook. Use nouns from the reading in Practice A. Underline all the nouns.

Example: My <u>sister</u> is a <u>senior</u> in <u>high school</u>.

Practice C: Write three sentences in your notebook. Use verbs from the reading in Practice A. Underline all the verbs.

Example: I <u>talk</u> to my guidance counselor every week.

SEE PAGE 195 FOR ANSWERS.

Identify Correct Verb Tenses and Verb Forms

Verb Tense

A **verb** tells what a noun or pronoun *is* or *does*.

All sentences have a **main verb**. Some sentences have a **helping verb**, too.

Example: Paul plays basketball every day.

> Main verb: *plays*

He is playing now.

> Main verb: *playing*   Helping verb: *is*

He has played basketball for many years.

> Main verb: *played*   Helping verb: *has*

> **TIP**
>
> The verbs *be, have,* and *do* and their forms are important helping verbs.

Read the sentences. Underline the <u>helping verb</u> once. Underline the <u>main verb</u> twice.

Example: People <u>have</u> <u>returned</u> over $23 million worth of items to Tokyo's lost-and-found center.

A. Umbrellas, cell, phones, and money were put in neat piles at the center.

B. Many women have lost their handbags.

C. A lost diamond ring was stored in a special bin.

D. People have lost more cell phones than other kinds of objects.

A. <u>were</u> <u>put</u>; B. <u>have</u> <u>lost</u>; C. <u>was</u> <u>stored</u>; D. <u>have</u> <u>lost</u>

Verbs also show *time*, or tense, in a sentence. The verb tense can be in the past, present, or future.

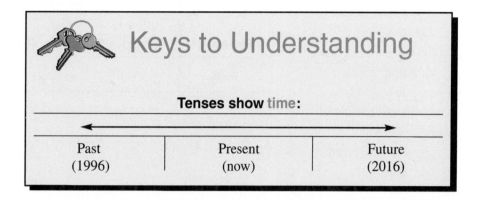

Read the sentences below. Look at the underlined verbs. Do they show past, present, or future time? Write the verbs in the correct column below.

I <u>walk</u> to school with my friends in the morning.

We <u>waved</u> to the students on the bus.

I <u>will go</u> to a club after school.

We <u>played</u> spelling games yesterday.

I <u>am learning</u> good writing skills.

We <u>are going to pass</u> a writing test.

Past	Present	Future
	walk	

Past: waved, played; Present: am learning;
Future: will go, are going to pass

Regular Verbs

You already know a lot about verbs:

• Verbs tell what nouns or pronouns do or are.

• Verbs sometimes have helping verbs (a form of like *be, have,* or *do*).

• Verbs show time (tense).

Each verb also has four forms. These forms are used to show different tenses. Participles are used with helping verbs to create other tenses.

Present	Simple Past	Past Participle	Present Participle
walk	walked	walked	walking

Keys to Understanding

Form	Use
Simple Tenses	
Simple present base form of verb	• actions happening now *We look at this page.* • routines and general truths *We look at this book every day.*
Simple past base form + *-ed*	• actions that finished in the past *We looked at page 29 yesterday.*
Simple future *will* + base form	• actions that are going to happen in the future *We will look at page 31 next.*
Continuous Tenses for actions that continue over time	
Present continuous present form of *be* + present participle	*We are looking at page 30 right now.*
Past continuous past form of *be* + present participle	*We were looking at our books all morning.*
Future continuous *will* and *be* + present participle	*We will be looking at our homework tomorrow.*
Perfect Tenses for actions that finished at or before a specific time	
Present perfect present form of *have* + past participle	*We have looked at this page for ten minutes.*
Past perfect Past form of *have* + past participle	*We had looked at page 29 first.*
Future perfect *will* and *have* + past participle	*We will have looked at page 31 by tomorrow.*

Strategies for Test-Taking Success: Writing © Heinle, Cengage Learning. Photocopying this page is prohibited by law.

Read the sentences. Choose the correct form of the verb for the first sentence.

They _____ humpback whales from the Arctic to the Equator for many years. They learned a lot about the whales on their trips.

A. are following   B. followed   C. will follow

B is correct. The verb *learned* is in the past tense, so the scientists took their trips in the past. You need a past tense form. A is present continuous, and C is future.

Irregular Verbs

Regular verbs follow patterns to form the simple past:
like – liked   walk – walked

Irregular verbs don't follow patterns. Each simple past form needs to be learned: *be – was   go – went   do – did*

The forms of the verbs *be* and *have* are important to learn.

TIP

Use a form of *be* and the *present participle* to form the continuous tenses.

I *am playing.* She *was dancing.* They *will be watching.*

Use a form of *have* and the *past participle* to form the perfect tenses.

I *have played.* She *had danced.* They *have watched.*

Verb	Past	Past Participle	Present Participle
be	was were	been	being
have	had	had	having

Review tenses of *be* and *have*.

Present	Past	Present Perfect	Present Continuous
be			
(I) am	was	have <u>been</u>	am <u>being</u>
(you, we, they) are	were	have <u>been</u>	are <u>being</u>
(he, she, it) is	was	has <u>been</u>	is <u>being</u>
have			
(I) have	had	have <u>had</u>	am <u>having</u>
(you, we, they) have	had	have <u>had</u>	are <u>having</u>
(he, she, it) has	had	has <u>had</u>	is <u>having</u>

More Irregular Verbs			
	Simple Past	**Past Participle**	**Present Participle**
begin	began	begun	beginning
break	broke	broken	breaking
bring	brought	brought	bringing
come	came	come	coming
do	did	done	doing
eat	ate	eaten	eating
get	got	gotten	getting
give	gave	given	giving
go	went	gone	going
know	knew	known	knowing
leave	left	left	leaving
make	made	made	making
read	read	read	reading
ride	rode	ridden	riding
run	ran	run	running
see	saw	seen	seeing
take	took	taken	taking
write	wrote	written	writing

Practice A: Read the sentences. Write *P* for past, *R* for present, or *F* for future time.

Example: R Pluto is the smallest planet in our solar system.

___ 1. Pluto was first seen in 1930.

___ 2. Pluto is usually the ninth planet from the sun after Neptune, the eighth planet.

___ 3. Every 248 years, Neptune and Pluto change places for 20 years.

___ 4. They will change places again in 2247.

Practice B: Write the correct form of the verb.

Example: (see, were seen) In American films before the 1970s, Asian Americans *were seen* as weak.

(changed, was changing) 1. Bruce Lee _____ all that with his kung fu films.

(take, took) 2. Lee _____ his first martial arts class in his teens.

(is called, is calling) 3. His style of kung fu _____ "jeet kune do."

(allows, allowing) 4. It _____ a person to fight with fast kicks and punches.

(was making, made) 5. It _____ him a star in the United States.

(showed, will show) 6. It also _____ Asian Americans as strong and smart.

(will be remembering, will be remembered) 7. Bruce Lee _____ for his strength, creativity, and talent.

Practice C: Complete these sentences with information about yourself. Use the past, present, or future tense.

1. At age five, I _____

_____

2. Now I _____

_____

3. In five years, I _____

_____

SEE PAGE 195 FOR ANSWERS AND EXPLANATIONS.

Recognize Mistakes in Subject–Verb Agreement

Recognize Subjects

The **subject** is who or what the sentence is about.

Justina is pretty.

This sentence is about Justina. So *Justina* is the subject.

Manuel and Chan are good students.

This sentence is about Manuel and Chan. So *Manuel and Chan* are the subjects.

We have a new teacher in Room 4.

This sentence is about us (*we*). So *we* is the subject.

Underline the subjects in these sentences.

Example: Six <u>students</u> are running for class president.

    A. Franz wants to have more school dances.

    B. Amalia wants to improve school lunches.

    C. One student hasn't made a speech.

    D. Wing-Li and Doris want to be co-presidents.

    E. Last year's president wants to run again, too.

A. Franz; B. Amalia; C. student; D. Wing-Li and Doris;
E. president

Subject–Verb Agreement

Subject–verb agreement means that **subjects** and **verbs** have to match. Subjects and verbs must match in number (singular or plural). They must match in person (1st, 2nd, or 3rd), too.

	Singular	**Plural**
1st person	I	we
2nd person	you (1 person)	you (2 or more people)
3rd person	he, she, it	they

Strategies for Test-Taking Success: Writing © Heinle, Cengage Learning. Photocopying this page is prohibited by law.

TIPS

1. Sometimes it's hard to know if a subject is singular or plural. Try using a pronoun for the noun.

Mike (*he*) runs every day.

Mario and Conchita (*they*) are on the track team, too.

2. For *he, she,* and *it*: verbs in the present tense end in *-s*.

I like fruit. She likes milk.

TIP

Be careful with *There is* and *There are*:

There is a new teacher in Room 4.

This is about one teacher; use a singular verb, *is*.

There are many new students in my class.

This is about many students. Use a plural verb, *are*.

 Keys to Understanding

To make subjects and verbs agree:

• use *singular verbs* with *singular subjects*.

I train with my track team.

Mike runs every day.

He is training for the track meet.

• use *plural verbs* with *plural subjects*

Mario and Conchita have a track team at their school, too.

They run from their school to the river and back.

They have run 2 miles every day since September.

Check the sentence in which the subject and verb agree.

___ A. William Boyle is the inventor of the credit card.

___ B. It were invented at the Franklin National Bank in 1951.

You are correct if you picked A. The subject *William Boyle* is singular. The verb *is* is singular. In B, the pronoun *It* is singular, but the verb *were* is plural.

Practice A: Underline the subject of each sentence. Write **S** for singular subjects. Write **P** for plural subjects. Then circle the correct verb.

Example: <u>*P* Snowmobiles</u> (is, (are)) very popular in cold places.

___ 1. You (drive, drives) them on snowy trails in the woods.

___ 2. Some states (have, has) an age requirement for driving a snowmobile.

___ 3. A snowmobile (make, makes) a lot of noise.

___ 4. The noise (scare, scares) wild animals.

___ 5. Some people (want, wants) to limit the number of snowmobiles in parks.

Practice B: Look at the underlined verbs in the paragraph. Correct any verbs that don't agree with their subjects.

> *wear*
>
> Most people <u>~~wears~~</u> blue jeans. But <u>have</u> you ever wondered who *Jean* was? In fact, Jean <u>was</u> not a person at all. It <u>were</u> a place. It used to be spelled *g-e-n-e*. It <u>was</u> named for the blue cotton cloth made in Genoa, Italy. So there you <u>has</u> it. Jeans is a changed word. The word <u>come</u> all the way from Genoa.

Practice C: Write five sentences in your notebook. Write about something that happened at your school last week. Underline the subjects and the verbs. Make sure that the subjects and verbs agree.

Example: Last week, a <u>speaker</u> <u>came</u> to our school.

SEE PAGE 195 FOR ANSWERS AND EXPLANATIONS.

Strategy 6

Recognize Problems with Pronouns

Make Sure Pronouns Replace Nouns

It's important for a reader to know what noun a pronoun is replacing. The noun (person, place, thing, or idea) has to be clear.

She plays basketball. She is working on her jump shot.

Who is the subject of these sentences? You don't know. You don't know which noun *she* replaces.

Now read this change.

> **TIP**
>
> Be sure to put the noun first and the pronoun after it.

Mai plays basketball. She is working on her jump shot.

Now the noun is clear. The pronoun *she* replaces *Mai*.

Check the sentence that has a pronoun without a clear noun.

____ A. Megan wants to join the team. But she thinks that she is too short.

____ B. He tells Megan not to worry. He knows that she's fast.

Who is *He*? Is *he* the coach? Is *he* Megan's brother? Is *he* a friend? You can't tell. B is the correct answer. B needs a noun to tell you who the pronoun *He* is.

1. Don't put a lot of words between a noun and its pronoun. Make sure your reader knows which noun the pronoun replaces.

> Tennis is Raffi's favorite sport. He has a strong serve, but his backhand needs work. He learned how to do it when he was a kid.

What noun does *it* replace? Did Raffi learn *tennis* or his *backhand* when he was a kid? You can't be sure.

Now read this change.

> Tennis is Raffi's favorite sport. He learned to play it when he was a kid. He has a strong serve, but his backhand needs work.

The pronoun, *it*, is close to its noun, *tennis*. Now there is no confusion.

2. Watch out for pronouns that can replace more than one noun.

> There are special tools that shop teachers use for cutting wood. They are helpful when you need a a sign.

Does *They* mean *special tools* or *shop teachers*? It's hard to be sure. To fix this problem, repeat the noun.

> There are special tools that shop teachers use for cutting wood. The special tools are helpful when you need a sign.

Underline the pronoun problem in each sentence. Circle the nouns that those pronouns might replace.

Example: In shop class, we use wooden (rods) to make CD (racks). <u>They</u> are very useful.

A. Moustafa put his CD rack on his desk. It is very well made.

B. The music teacher has four CD racks. She puts them in the music rooms. They are for her band classes.

A. Underline *It*. This word is a problem because it might mean his *CD rack* or his *desk*. B. Underline *They*. This pronoun might mean *CD racks* or *music rooms*.

Use the Right Pronoun

Nouns and pronouns must match in *three* ways at the same time. They must match in:

- **number**
  singular: Joe loves baseball. He plays every year.
  plural: My brother and sister love soccer. They play every day.

- **person**
  1st: My brother and I like computers. We are on the Robot Team.
  2nd: You and Pablo are my classmates. You are my friends, too.
  3rd: The school bus is coming. It is down the street.

- **gender**
  male: Mr. Albert is the coach. He is a great teacher.
  female: Ms. Marcos plays soccer. She is a goalie.
  neuter: The team won a medal. It is silver.

> **TIP**
>
> Neuter means something is not a male or a female. Most nouns in English are neuter.

Write the pronouns that agree with the underlined nouns.

Example: <u>Marianna</u> went camping with (her, their) <u>her</u> parents last summer.

A. They camped in the Smoky Mountains National <u>Park</u>.
   (He, It) _____ was beautiful.

B. <u>Her parents</u> cooked over a fire. (Their, Her) _____ dinner was delicious.

A. *It. Park* is a 3rd person, singular, neuter noun.
B. *Their. Parents* is a 3rd person, plural noun.

Practice A: Read the story. Write the correct pronouns. Use the context of the story to help you choose the correct pronouns.

The Bulky Lizard

In 1858, William Foulke was on vacation in New Jersey. (He, It) <u>He</u> heard about some gigantic bones nearby. He said to his wife, "(She, You) 1. _____ will be amazed. (I, They) 2. _____ am going to put all the bones together." (They, We) 3. _____ formed a strange animal. (She, It) 4. _____ was bigger than an elephant and looked like a lizard and a bird. Foulke had discovered the first nearly complete dinosaur skeleton. (Its, His) 5. _____ name was Hadrosaurus. Scientists were amazed. (They, You) 6. _____ came from all around the world to see this "bulky lizard."

Practice B: Each sentence below has a problem pronoun. Underline it. Then write the correct sentences in your notebook. Change the verb forms if needed.

Example: Students need fiber in <u>your</u> diets.
<u>Students need fiber in their diets.</u>

1. Fresh fruit has fiber. They are in grains, too.

2. Try to eat apples at lunch. You are 15¢ each.

3. You can buy pears, bananas, and berries in the cafeteria, too. They are all good choices for our lunch.

SEE PAGE 195 FOR ANSWERS AND EXPLANATIONS.

Adjectives tell about *nouns*. Adjectives describe nouns and add details. Adjectives make your writing interesting.

The trees are tall.

Several tall trees are next to the road.

Adjectives also compare nouns.

To compare nouns, add *-er* or *-est* to most adjectives.

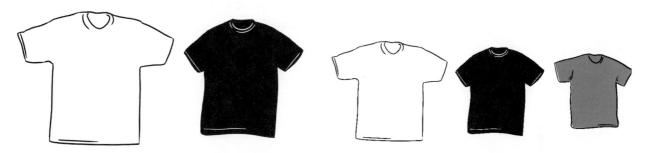

The black shirt is smaller than the white shirt.   The blue shirt is the smallest of all.

TIPS

1. Never use -er with more. Never use -est with most.

    ~~more~~ greener

    most beautiful~~est~~

2. *Good* is an adjective. It describes the subject.

    The music is good.

    Well is an adverb. It describes the verb.

    He plays the trumpet well.

 Keys to Understanding

For *short* adjectives, add *-er* and *-est*.
For *long* adjectives, use *more* and *most* before the adjective.

	Adjective	Comparing 2 Items	Comparing 3 or More Items
short	tall	taller than	the tallest
long	beautiful	more beautiful than	the most beautiful
Important *irregular* adjectives	good	better	best
	bad	worse	worst
	far	farther	farthest

Check the correct sentence.

___ A. My chair is most comfortable than your chair.

___ B. Pink roses are the most fragrant[1] flowers of all.

B is correct. A compares two chairs.
So the correct way to write it is *more comfortable than.*

Practice A: Read these sentences. Fill in the correct form of the adjective.

Example: (strong) Mary is a <u>strong</u> girl.

(small) 1. Baby Juri is the _____ person in their house.
(good) 2. Mother is the _____ person in the world.
(old) 3. Dad is _____ Uncle Frank.
(beautiful) 4. Grandmother is the _____ person I know.
(handsome) 5. My brother is _____ a movie star.

Practice B: Compare Manuel and Aldo. Write five to ten sentences in your notebook. Use these adjectives and others you know.

old	fast	handsome	short

Example: <u>Aldo is taller than Manuel.</u>

SEE PAGE 195 FOR ANSWERS AND EXPLANATIONS.

[1] smells sweet

CHAPTER 2: REVIEW TEST

Review the steps in the process of elimination and test-taking strategies on pages 15–18. Then use these strategies to take a Chapter Review Test.

Mark your answers on the Answer Grid.

Read the story "My Pets." Choose the word or words that correctly answer Questions 1 through 5.

My Pets

I (1) _____ three pets: a duck, a parrot, and a dog. Scotty is a black and white duck. It tickles when he (2) _____ corn from my hand. He is the (3) _____ of my pets. The parrot is named Greeny. Guess what color he is! He sits on a perch and is (4) _____. Bobby is a poodle with curly black hair. He chases the duck. (5) _____ run in circles. Bobby barks at the parrot, too. He loves to play and tease. My pets are all special.

---

1 Which answer should go in blank (1)?

   A has

   B have

   C had

   D having

2 Which answer should go in blank (2)?

   A eat

   B ate

   C eats

   D had eaten

3 Which answer should go in blank (3)?

   A cute

   B cuter

   C cutest

   D most cutest

4 Which answer should go in blank (4)?

   A serious

   B seriouser

   C more serious

   D most serious than

5 Which answer should go in blank (5)?

   A He

   B You

   C Scotty

   D They

GO ON

Louise Thaden, Flying Ace

(1) She learned to fly airplanes in the 1920s. (2) Women didn't race against men in those days. (3)Women had your own races. (4) Louise Thaden won the first Women's Air Derby in 1929. (5) She didn't have computers to help. (6) She used roadmaps and a good sense of direction.

(7) Women finally flew against men in the 1936 Bendix Cup Race. (8) The race was from New York to California. (9) The prize were $5,000.

(10) "No woman can win our race," said the people from Bendix. (11) "But we don't want them to feel bad. (12) We had given them a prize of their own." (13) It was $2,000.

(14) Soon everyone was shocked. (15) Thaden and her co-pilot landed first. (16) They won all $7,000. (17) They set the record for most fast time for the race. (18) Another woman, Laura Ingalls, is coming in second place.

(19) "We had to prove that women were as good pilots as men," said Thaden. (20) Back then, many people didn't want women to drive a horse and cart, much less an automobile or an airplane. (21) So it was a big job to prove that women could pilot airplanes.

---

6 What is the correct way to write sentence 1?

  A Louise Thaden learned to fly airplanes in the 1920s.

  B She is learning to fly airplanes in the 1920s.

  C She learned flying airplanes in the 1920s.

  D Make no change.

7 What change, if any, should be made in sentence 3?

  A Change *had* to *have.*

  B Change *your* to *their.*

  C Change *own races* to *them.*

  D Make no change.

8 What change, if any, should be made in sentence 9?

  A Change *The prize* to *It.*

  B Insert *it* after *prize.*

  C Change *were* to *was.*

  D Make no change.

9 What change, if any, should be made in sentence 12?

  A Delete[2] *had.*

  B Change *had given* to *gave.*

  C Change *had given* to *will give.*

  D Make no change.

[2] take out

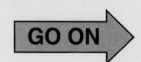
GO ON

Strategies for Test-Taking Success: Writing © Heinle, Cengage Learning. Photocopying this page is prohibited by law.

10   What change, if any, should be made in sentence 15?

    A   Change *landed* to *was landing*.

    B   Change *landed* to *lands*.

    C   Change *landed* to *are landing*.

    D   Make no change.

11   Choose the best word or phrase for the underlined part of sentence 17.

    They set the record for <u>most fast</u> time for the race.

    A   the fastest

    B   more fastest

    C   most fastest

    D   most faster

12   What change, if any, should be made in sentence 18?

    A   Change *is coming* to *came*.

    B   Change *is coming* to *come*.

    C   Change *is coming* to *was coming*.

    D   Make no change.

**STOP. THIS IS THE END OF THE REVIEW TEST.
SEE PAGE 195 FOR ANSWERS AND EXPLANATIONS.**

3

Use Spelling and Mechanics

Strategies for Test-Taking Success: Writing © Heinle, Cengage Learning. Photocopying this page is prohibited by law.

Strategy 8

Use Spelling Rules

You can spell many English words by matching sounds to letters.

You can spell other words by learning a few rules.

IE or *EI*? a Spelling Poem

This poem helps explain how to spell words with *ie* and *ei*.

TIP

When *ei* sounds like *a*, it is often followed by a silent *-gh* or *-gn*.

sleigh

reign

Poem	Example
Use *i* before *e*,	believe
except after *c*,	receive
or when it sounds like a	
as in neighbor or weigh.	sounds like: NAY-bur or WAY

Cross out the misspelled word.

Example: receive   relief   eight   ~~beleif~~

believe   achieve   theif   neighborhood

The poem says: *i* comes before *e*. So you are correct if you crossed out *theif*.

A **root** is the main part of a word. A **suffix** is added to the end of a root.

Slowly is made of a root and a suffix.

Sometimes you need to change the spelling of the root when you add a suffix to make a new word.

Roots change only when you add **vowel suffixes** (*-able, -er, -es, -est, -ed, -ily, -ing*).

Use the following spelling rules to check your writing.

1. For words ending in **silent** *-e*:

    Remove the *-e* before you add the suffix.

    love → loving   loved   lovable

2. For words ending in a **consonant** + *y*:

    Change the *-y* to *-i* and then add the suffix.

    study → studies   heavy → heavier   early → earliest
    EXCEPT: when the suffix is *-ing*   cry   crying

3. For words ending in **consonant + vowel + consonant**:

    Double the last consonant and then add the suffix.

    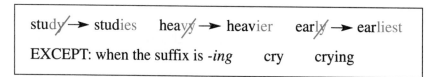

Strategies for Test-Taking Success: Writing © Heinle, Cengage Learning. Photocopying this page is prohibited by law.

Sometimes **roots do change.** Use the following spelling rules to check your writing.

1. For **consonant suffixes** (-*ful*, -*less*, -*ly*, -*ment*):
Do not change the spelling of the root.

care ⟶ care ful   fear ⟶ fear less   sad ⟶ sad ly

content ⟶ content ment

2. For words ending in a **vowel + -*y***:
Do not change the spelling of the root.

play ⟶ pl aying   monkey ⟶ monk eys   annoy ⟶ ann oyed

Find and underline the misspelled word.

Example:

My brother is the <u>happyest</u> boy I know.
It's upsetting to see ageing parents who are unemployed.

The word *ageing* is misspelled. Check rule #1 if you aren't sure why.
Check rule #3 if you underlined *upsetting*. Check rule #5 if
you underlined *unemployed*.

Forming Plurals

Add -*s* to make most nouns plural; add -*es* to nouns that end in -*ch*,
-*s*, -*sh*, and -*x*.

pie ⟶ pie s   boy ⟶ boy s   banana ⟶ banana s

ben ch ⟶ ben ches   clas s ⟶ clas ses   bo x ⟶ box es

Add -*s* to nouns ending in vowel + -*o*; add -*es* to nouns ending in
consonant + -*o*.

radio ⟶ radio s   hero ⟶ hero es

Make a Spelling Study Chart

Keep a list of words you often misspell. Set aside time to study a few words every day.

Make a Spelling Study Chart like the one below. In columns 1 and 2, write each word and its meaning. Then write the spelling rule for the word in the "Rule" column. Check the last column when you can spell the word.

Word	Meaning	Rule	Know
neighborhood	person who lives next door	The order is *ei* when the letters sound like AY	✓
studios	places where artists work	Add -s to nouns that end in a vowel + -o.	

How to study spelling words using your Spelling Study Chart:

1. Look at a word. Say it aloud. Try to "see" it in your mind.

2. Tap the number of syllables as you say the word.

3. Copy the word on another piece of paper as you repeat it.

4. Say each syllable. Write the whole syllable as you say it.

5. Cover the word. Then uncover each syllable as you read the word. Write each syllable again as you say it.

6. Put a check mark in the "Know" column when you know how to spell the word correctly.

For correct spelling: Cover the word. Write it on paper again.

For incorrect spelling: Repeat steps 1–6.

Strategies for Test-Taking Success: Writing © Heinle, Cengage Learning. Photocopying this page is prohibited by law.

Practice A: Cross out the misspelled word in each line. Then write it correctly.

~~funier~~	hitting	tried	_funnier_
1. refered	fitting	mopped	_____
2. movement	moveing	movable	_____
3. happyer	braking	valuable	_____
4. videos	dishes	tomatos	_____

Practice B: Use the root and suffix in parentheses to make a new word.

(love + ed) Barbara Rice _loved_ her job testing new video games.

(begin + ing)   1. At the _____ of each work day, she checked the bugs or problems in the software.

(try + ed)   2. Then she _____ to fix the bugs.

(enjoy + able)   3. The most _____ part of her day came next.

(happy + est)   4. "I'm _____ when I'm playing video games," said Barbara.

(Make + ing)   5. "_____ games better is fun for me."

(attach + ment)   6. Barbara has a great _____ to her job.

SEE PAGE 196 FOR ANSWERS AND EXPLANATIONS.

Recognize Commonly Confused Words

Homonyms

Homonyms are words that sound alike. But they have different meanings and different spellings. That can be confusing. You need to read the whole sentence to figure out the meaning of the word.

The words *hear* and *here* sound the same. *Hear* means "to listen." But *here* means "this place."

Read the conversations. Are they correct?

1. **A:** Do you *hear* the birds?

   B: Yes. Their chirping makes a happy sound.

2. **C:** Is it far to the library?

   D: No. It's right *here*.

The conversations are both correct. Conversation 1 has two hints: chirping and sound. In conversation 2, here tells you that the people are at the library.

On the next page you will find a list of common homonyms to learn.

Homonyms	Meanings	Examples
brake	to slow down or stop	Cars *brake* when the traffic light is yellow.
break	to damage or crack;	*Break* the egg into a hot frying pan.
	time to rest	I usually have a snack during my *break*.
hour	60 minutes	It's 11:00 a.m. Lunch starts in an *hour*.
our	belonging to us	I live here with my family. This is *our* house.
its	belonging to it	The dog played with *its* ball.
it's	*it + is*	*It's* a red rubber ball.
knew	past form of *know*	I *knew* how to multiply in the 4th grade.
new	latest, not old	My bike is too small. I need a *new* one.
know	to understand	I *know* how to drive.
no	reject/negative	*No*. I don't have a car.
passed	went by	I *passed* all the other runners!
	succeeded	The whole class *passed* the English test.
past	a time before	History is the study of *past* events.
peace	calm, quiet/no war	The war ended. Now the country is at *peace*.
piece	part, section	Do you want a *piece* of fruit?
right	correct	Is that the *right* answer?
	opposite of left	Start marching with your *right* foot.
write	put words on paper	I have to *write* a paper for history class.
their	belonging to them	My cousins live here. This is *their* house.
there	in that place	Sign your name *there*, at the bottom of the form.
they're	*they + are*	I like Leila and Tran. *They're* my friends from gym class.
to	toward	Mohammed is going *to* the library.
too	also	Jack is going, *too*.
two	number 2	The *two* boys will study together.
weather	climate	The *weather* is hot today. It's 90°.
whether	if	Ask *whether* you can study at my house.
weak	not strong	I am sick and feel *weak*.
week	seven days	The first *week* of school is exciting.
wear	put on clothes	I like to *wear* my school sweater.
where	in what place?	*Where* is your next class?
who's	*who + is*	*Who's* your math teacher this year?
whose	belonging to which person	*Whose* book is this?
your	belonging to you	Is this *your* science book?
you're	*you + are*	*You're* right on time.

Other Words Often Confused

These words aren't homonyms, but they are often confused. Learn their different meanings. Read the whole sentence to understand the context. Then they won't confuse you.

Words	Meaning	Example
accept	to agree or take	Please *accept* this gift with our thanks.
except	all but	I like all my teachers *except* Mr. Howell.
affect	to influence	The weather usually *affects* my mood.
effect	result	One *effect* of polluted water is sick fish.
among	use with three or more	I divided the pizza *among* my five friends.
between	use with two	I can't choose *between* Mary and Alice.
than	use in comparisons	History class is longer *than* band practice.
then	shows time	First, I study. *Then*, I practice my drums.
we're	*we + are*	*We're* taking an English test today.
were	past form of *are* for *you, we, they*	We *were* studying together.
quiet	not noisy	My street is very *quiet* on Sunday morning.
quite	very	The weather was *quite* warm yesterday.

Practice A: Write the correct word on the line.

My grandmother lives (to / too / two) <u>too</u> far away (to / too / two) (1) _____ visit every (weak / week) (2) _____. But she wants to (know / no) (3) _____ everything that's going on. She asks, "How's the (weather / whether) (4) _____? (Its / It's) (5) _____ hot again, right?" "(Who's / Whose) (6) _____ visiting Uncle Don?" "What will you (wear / where) (7) _____ to cousin Marthe's wedding?" "Is Joan taller (than / then) (8) _____ her mother?"

(Hour / Our) (9) _____ family sent letters in the (passed / past) (10) _____. But now (we're / were) (11) _____ sending e-mails. (Their / There / They're) (12) _____ very fast. Grandmother loves them.

How do you communicate with (your / you're) (13) _____ relatives?

Practice B: Write six sentences in your notebook. Use words from the lists of homonymns and other words often confused.

<u>This is where I live.</u>

SEE PAGE 196 FOR ANSWERS AND EXPLANATIONS.

Strategies for Test-Taking Success: Writing © Heinle, Cengage Learning. Photocopying this page is prohibited by law.

Identify Proper Nouns

A noun names a person, place, thing, or idea. A proper noun names a specific person, place, thing, or idea. A proper noun always starts with a capital, or uppercase, letter.

TIP

Don't capitalize *the* before a proper noun. *the* White House

Noun	Proper Noun
girl	Marianna
president	President John F. Kennedy
city	Chicago
building	the Empire State Building

Underline the proper nouns. Rewrite them with capital letters.

classmates   <u>janet</u>   <u>Janet</u>

state _____
holiday _____
arizona _____
dr. diaz _____
election day _____
miami _____
new jersey _____
country _____
the golden gate bridge _____
the fourth of july _____

The proper nouns are *Arizona, Dr. Diaz, Election Day, Miami, New Jersey*, the *Golden Gate Bridge*, and *the Fourth of July*.

Use Capitalization Rules

Always use a capital letter for the pronoun *I* and the first letter of the first word of a sentence.

Good writers also use capital letters for:

1. people's names, including titles, initials, and abbreviations

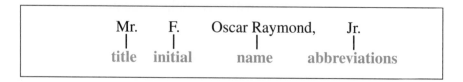

2. names on maps, including streets, towns, cities, states, countries, bodies of water, mountains, islands, and so on.

| West Street | San Diego | Florida | China |
| the Caribbean | the Atlantic Ocean | | the Andes |

TIP

Don't capitalize the names of the seasons.

spring, winter

3. days, months, and holidays

| Wednesday | January | Thanksgiving Day |

TIP

Don't capitalize regular school subjects.

science, math, history

UNLESS they are proper nouns or course names.

English, Advanced Spanish, Math 101; Introduction to Computer Science, World History

4. languages, religions, nationalities, and ethnic groups

| English | Hindu | Haitian | the Kurds |

Check the address that has correct capitalization.

____ A.

Mr. and ms. Rudy Stone
1566 First Avenue
New York, NY

____ B.

Hispanic Institute
La Rambla 301
Ponce, PR

____ C.

Dr. Lee N. Chang
455 maple road
Dallas, TX

You are correct if you checked B. In A, *ms.* is a title and an abbreviation. It starts with a capital letter. In C, *maple road* is a street name. Street names start with capital letters.

Strategies for Test-Taking Success: Writing © Heinle, Cengage Learning. Photocopying this page is prohibited by law.

Practice A: Check the words that need capital letters. Then rewrite them correctly on the line.

✓ tuesday _Tuesday_

___ 1. j.k. rowling _____

___ 2. a long river _____

___ 3. jewish _____

___ 4. may 17th _____

___ 5. native american _____

___ 6. spanish _____

___ 7. the great salt lake _____

___ 8. the seashore _____

___ 9. tom _____

___ 10. yesterday _____

Practice B: Rewrite the letter below in your notebook. Add capitals where needed.

> 🍎 **MEDGAR EVERS HIGH SCHOOL**
>
> **evers high school**
> **1234 Main Street**
> **san antonio, texas 78249**
>
> Dear mr. brand,
>
>   thank you for the tour of the witte museum in san antonio. Our class is studying animal habitats in texas ecology 101. it was exciting to see the different ways that animals live in our state.
>
>   we also loved the h.e.b. science treehouse near the san antonio river.
>
>   thank you again for your time and help. we hope to return to the witte museum again soon.
>
> Sincerely,
> mrs. green's texas ecology 101 class
> evers secondary school

Practice C: Think about the names of people, places, and holidays you know. Complete this chart with proper nouns.

People	Places	Holidays
Abraham Lincoln		

SEE PAGE 197 FOR ANSWERS AND EXPLANATIONS.

Use Correct Punctuation

Use Correct End Marks

There are three ways to end a sentence.

1. Most sentences are statements. A statement ends with a period (.).

   Fourscore and seven years ago our fathers brought forth upon this continent, a new nation, conceived in Liberty, and dedicated to the proposition that all men are created equal.

   —Abraham Lincoln

2. A question ends with a question mark (?).

   Romeo, Romeo, wherefore art thou, Romeo?

   —William Shakespeare

3. Exclamations are sentences that show surprise or strong feeling. An exclamation ends with an exclamation point (!).

   One small step for a man, one giant leap for mankind!

   —Neil Armstrong

Check the sentence with the correct end punctuation.

___ A. Let's get some CDs?

___ B. Is Marcy meeting us at the store.

___ C. I can't believe she's late again!

You are correct if you checked C. The sentence is an exclamation. It shows strong emotion. A is a statement. Like most sentences, it should end with a period. B is a direct question. It needs a question mark.

Practice A: Read the sentences. Mark the circle that describes the sentence.

	Statement	Question	Exclamation
How do I get to Main Street?	(S)	**(Q)**	(E)
1. Go left at the corner.	(S)	(Q)	(E)
2. Could you say that again, please?	(S)	(Q)	(E)
3. Do I pass the library?	(S)	(Q)	(E)
4. Yes.	(S)	(Q)	(E)
5. Main Street is the next street.	(S)	(Q)	(E)
6. Thank you so much!	(S)	(Q)	(E)

Practice B: Write *C* for sentences with correct end punctuation. Write *I* for sentences with incorrect end punctuation.

Example:

_C_ What is a blog?

_I_ A blog is a we*b log* on the Internet!

___ 1. A blog is a journal or story?

___ 2. You can find tools on the Internet.

___ 3. Does it cost a lot to have a personal blog!

___ 4. Some software for creating blogs is free.

___ 5. But watch out?

___ 6. Sometimes software costs a lot.

___ 7. You can edit, or change, your blog!

___ 8. Click the "Publish" button to put your blog on the Internet?

Practice C: Rewrite the incorrect sentences from Practice B in your notebook. Correct the punctuation.

A blog is a web log on the Internet.

SEE PAGE 197 FOR ANSWERS AND EXPLANATIONS.

1. Use a comma to separate days, dates, and years.

   Monday, June 3, 2008

2. Use a comma between a city and a state or a country.

   River City, Iowa   London, England

3. Use a comma in large numbers to count off groups of three digits.

1,000	one thousand
1,000,000	one million
1,000,000,000	one billion
1,000,000,000,000	one trillion

4. Use a comma to separate three or more items in a series.

          1   2   3
   My favorite subjects are math, English, and biology.

5. Use a comma and a conjunction (*and, but, for, nor, yet, or, so*) to connect two complete sentences. This is a good way to combine ideas.[2]

   Jan wants to save for a computer. She is working in the library.

   Jan wants to save for a computer, so she is working in the library.

6. Use a comma to separate the introductory words from the main sentence.

Introductory Words	Complete sentence
Yes,	it is a tropical climate.
During the day,	the temperature is very high.
For example,	it was over 94° every day this week.

[1] There's more practice with commas in Chapter 4.
[2] Learn more about combining sentences on pages 74–75.

Check the sentence that uses commas correctly.

____ A. Isidro usually drinks milk water, or juice.

____ B. Isidro has fruit for breakfast, and he eats pasta for dinner.

____ C. Isidro also likes salad, and tomato sauce.

B is correct. It connects two complete thoughts with a comma + *and*. A needs a comma after *milk* to separate three items in a series. The comma in C is unnecessary. That series has only two items.

Practice A: Read the sentences below. Underline the part of the sentence that uses commas. Write the words from the box that describe how the comma is used in each sentence.

(Hint: Some sentences use commas in two ways.)

large number	date	series	comma and conjunction	~~introductory words~~

<u>Located between Canada and the United States,</u> Niagara Falls was created by the last Ice Age. <u>introductory words</u>

1. Niagara Falls is made up of three falls: the American Falls, the Bridal Veil Falls, and the Horseshoe Falls. _____

2. The Niagara River is about 12,000 years old, but the modern Niagara Falls is much younger. _____

3. Water flow in the Niagara River is heaviest in June, July, and August. _____

4. Water flow is lightest in winter, so the river sometimes freezes. _____

5. An ice jam stopped the falls for several hours on March 29, 1848, and an electric company stopped the American Falls for several months in 1969. _____

6. Until 1912, visitors walked or drove sleds over the ice in winter. _____

7. Today, about 12,000,000 tourists visit Niagara Falls each year. _____

Practice B: Read the story. Add commas where they are needed.

Hint: Not every sentence needs a comma.

Louis Braille, Teenage Inventor

Louis Braille was born on January 4, 1809. Before the age of 16 the French boy invented a way for blind people to read and write. As a child Louis Braille was blinded in an accident. He went to school but he only listened. The teachers didn't know how to teach him reading writing or math.

Then in 1821 Louis met a soldier named Charles Barbier. The man had invented a way to read and write in the dark. He called it "night writing." He knew night writing could help blind people. It used 12 raised dots and it helped soldiers send messages silently. Louis improved Barbier's invention. The teenager made the code easier. He cut the number of dots from 12 to 6. In 1829 Louis printed the first Braille book.

Thanks to a teenage inventor blind children can read write and learn any subject they want. The young French boy's invention makes elevators and public places safer for blind people.

SEE PAGE 198 FOR ANSWERS AND EXPLANATIONS.

Use Apostrophes

Use an **apostrophe** (') with contractions and possessives.

For **contractions**: The apostrophe shows where words are combined and letters are removed.

Most contractions combine a pronoun and a verb.

I + ~~have~~ = I've   she + ~~is~~ = she's   they + ~~will~~ = they'll

Sometimes contractions combine a verb and *not*.

is + not = isn't   cannot = can't   was + not = wasn't

For **possessives**: Add *'s* to a noun to show ownership.

This is Alphonse's book. (The book belongs to Alphonse.)

The lamp's light bulb is broken. (The light bulb is part of the lamp.)

Some words with contractions sound like possessive pronouns. Make sure you choose the correct word when you write.

its ⟷ it's	The dog is hungry. (Its / It's) dish is empty.
	Does the long form *It is* work in this sentence? No. Then *Its* is correct.
your ⟷ you're	Is Ms. Gonzalez (your / you're) math teacher?
	Does the long form *you are* work in this sentence? No. Then *your* is correct.
their ⟷ they're	(Their/They're) in her class now.
	Does the long form *they are* work in this sentence? Yes. Then the contraction *They're* is correct.

TIP

To check whether a word is a possessive pronoun or a contraction, restate the sentence with the long form.

Its name is Fluffy. Does *It is* name is Fluffy make sense? If not, use the possessive pronoun, *its*.

 Keys to Understanding

These are possessive pronouns. Do NOT add *'s* to them.

my / mine	our / ours
your / yours	your / yours
his	their / theirs
her / hers	
its	

Check the sentence that uses apostrophes correctly.

___ A. This is Jamal's printer.

___ B. The ink is in it's cartridge.

___ C. But the cartridge do'esnt fit in the printer.

You are correct if you checked A. Try the long form of the contraction *it's* in sentence B. (The ink is in *it is* cartridge.) The contraction doesn't work. The apostrophe is in the wrong place in C.

Use Colons and Semicolons

Use a colon (:) in three main ways:

1. after the salutation in a formal or business letter

   To Whom It May Concern:

2. to separate hours from minutes

   9:30 a.m.

3. to introduce a list

   Please send the following students to the nurse's office for eye exams: Dolores Sanchez, Mimi Chao, Juri Redecha, and Milo Hernandez.

Use a semicolon[3] (;) to connect two complete sentences that are strongly related.

Our basketball team is the best in town; we beat Middletown High by 30 points.

Mirabel wants to win a scholarship; she studies very hard.

---

[3] Learn more about using semicolons to combine sentences on pages 74–75.

Check the sentence with correct punctuation.

___ A. Miguel took his parents to the science fair: he had a special experiment to show them.

___ B. Maya's parents met her at school; she stayed late to help out.

You are correct if you checked B. The semicolon connects two complete sentences that are related. A needs a semicolon instead of a colon.

Practice A: Write *C* for correct punctuation. Write *I* for incorrect punctuation. Correct the mistakes on the lines.

Example: <u>I</u> Their's teamwork made the captain's job easy.
<u>their</u>

___ 1. Its crew had many skills. _____

___ 2. Data was an android. His computer brain was like an encyclopedia. _____

___ 3. Lt. Worf was a Klingon. His's background made him a great fighter. _____

___ 4 Deanna Troi read peoples emotions. _____

Practice B: Read this letter. Add punctuation. Change spelling and capitalization as needed.

September 26 200_

To Whom It May Concern

Tickets for the drama clubs production of *The Music Man* will be available on Wednesday october 12 2005. Their will be performances on Friday Saturday and Sunday at 730 p.m. Tickets are $5. Come early seats are limited.

Support drama at you're school

Mr. Minigan

Drama Coach

SEE PAGE 198 FOR ANSWERS AND EXPLANATIONS.

Practice C: In your notebook write a letter about an event at your school. Check for correct spelling, capitalization, and punctuation.

CHAPTER 3: REVIEW TEST

Mark your answers on the Answer Grid.

Read this story. Then answer Questions 1 through 11.

Clever Rani

(1) Long ago in India, a rajah ruled a kingdom of rice farmers. Each year, the rajah took most of there rice. He promised to store the rice for the farmers. Then, it would be there when they needed it. For many years, the rice grew well. Then one year the rice didn't grow. The people were hungry. He begged the rajah to open the warehouses.

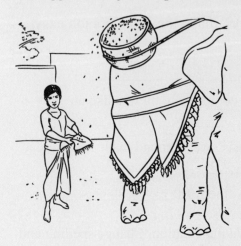

(2) "No," cried the rajah. "I must have the rice. Promise or no promise a rajah must not go hungry." So, his people starved.

(3) One day, the royal elephant brought two full baskets of rice to the palace. A girl named Rani saw some rice trickle from one of the baskets. She catches the rice in her scarf.

(4) A guard saw her and cried, "Stop, thief? You are stealing the rajah's rice."

(5) Rani quickly answered, "The rice fell from a basket: and I am returning it to His Highness."

(6) The rajah heard about the girl and wanted to reward her. "Ask me for anything," he said. "It will be your's."

(7) "All right, Your Highness," said Rani, who was very smart. "Today, give me one grain of rice. Then each day, for the next thirty days, give me twice as much rice as you gave me the day before. Tomorrow, you will give me two grains of rice. The next day, give me four grains of rice, and so on, for thirty days."

(8) The rajah thought the girl was a fool but he agreed to Ranis request. He handed her the first grain of rice.

(9) The next day, Rani got two grains of rice. The following day, she got four grains of rice. On the 9th day, Rani was presented with 256 grains of rice. Each day the amount of rice was doubled. By the 12th day, Rani recieved 2,048 grains of rice, or about four handfuls. On day 20, she got 16 bags of rice. On the 24th day, Rani received 8,388,608 grains of rice. It filled eight baskets and was carried by eight royal deer. On the 29th day, Rani was presented with the contents of the two royal storehouses. The rajah had no rice left, but he new Rani wasn't a fool.

(10) "What will you do with the rice?" he asked.

(11) "I'll give it to all the hungry people," said Rani. "I'll leave a basket for you, to. You must take only as much as you need, Your Highness." From then on, that's what he did.

—based on an Indian folktale

Strategies for Test-Taking Success: Writing © Heinle, Cengage Learning. Photocopying this page is prohibited by law.

1 Read this sentence from paragraph 1.

> Each year, the rajah took most of <u>there</u> rice.

What is the correct way to spell the underlined word?

A their

B theirs

C they're

D Make no change.

2 Choose the best word for the underlined part of paragraph 1.

> The people were hungry. <u>He</u> begged the rajah to open the warehouses.

A Our

B We

C They

D Make no change.

3 Which version of the sentence in paragraph 2 shows the correct place to put a comma?

A Promise, or no promise a rajah must not go hungry.

B Promise or no, promise a rajah must not go hungry.

C Promise or no promise, a rajah must not go hungry.

D Promise or no promise a rajah, must not go hungry.

4 What is the correct way to write the sentence from paragraph 3?

A She is catching the rice in her scarf.

B She caught the rice in her scarf.

C She will catch the rice in her scarf.

D Make no change.

5
> A guard saw her and cried, "Stop, thief?"

What change, if any, should be made to this sentence?

A Capitalize the *g* in *guard*.

B Change *cried* to *cryed*.

C Change *thief* to *theif*.

D Change the question mark to an exclamation point.

6 Read this sentence from paragraph 5.

> Rani quickly answered, "The rice fell from a <u>basket: and</u> I am returning it to His Highness."

What is the correct way to write the underlined words?

A basket and

B basket. And

C basket, and

D Make no change.

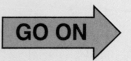

7

> It will be <u>your's</u>.

How should the underlined word in paragraph 6 be written?

A your

B yours

C you're

D Make no change.

8 **In which sentence below is all the punctuation correct?**

A The rajah thought the girl was a fool, but he agreed to Rani's request.

B The rajah thought the girl was a fool, but he agreed to Ranis' request.

C The rajah thought the girl was a fool? But he agreed to Rani's request.

D The rajah thought the girl was a fool! But he agreed to Ranis request.

9

> It filled eight baskets and was <u>carried</u> by eight royal deer.

What is the correct way to spell the underlined word?

A caried

B carryed

C carryied

D Make no change.

10

> The rajah had no rice left, but he new Rani wasn't a fool.

What change, if any, should be made to this sentence?

A Change the comma to a semicolon.

B Change *new* to *knew*.

C Delete the apostrophe in *wasn't*.

D Change the period to an exclamation point.

11

> "I'll leave a basket for you, to."

What change, if any, should be made to this sentence?

A Delete the apostrophe in *I'll*.

B Change *leave* to *leaving*.

C Change *to* to *too*.

D Change the period to a question mark.

GO ON ➡

For Questions 12 through 16, revise this form for a library card. Make corrections to capitalization and punctuation on the lines below each item on the form.

South branch public Library

South Branch Public Library

12   **Date:** october 22 2005

_____

13   **Name:** Joseph b. Marcos

_____

14   **Home Address:** 9614 north Market Street

_____

15   **City/State/Zip:** tallahassee FL 32329

_____

16   **School:** Washington street school

_____

STOP. THIS IS THE END OF THE REVIEW TEST.
SEE PAGE 198 FOR ANSWERS AND EXPLANATIONS.

Chapter 4 Write Sentences

Use Complete Sentences and Avoid Fragments

Recognize Complete Sentences

When you write, use complete sentences. Complete sentences have a subject and a verb.

A subject is *who* or *what* the sentence is about.

> Mr. Armstrong is a pilot. He flies jets.
>   subject   subject

A verb tells what the subject *is* or *does*.

> Mr. Armstrong is a pilot. He flies jets.
>   verb   verb

Complete sentences have everything they need to express a complete thought.

> **Complete:** Mr. Armstrong usually flies from San Diego to Houston.
> **Incomplete:** Sometimes flies from San Diego to Miami. (no subject)
> **Incomplete:** A pilot at Sunny Airlines for 12 years. (no verb)

Complete sentences have correct end punctuation.

Check the complete sentence.

___ A. My friend, Annamaria, and I.

___ B. She is the best friend in the world.

B is the complete sentence. A is missing a verb.
C is missing a subject.

Keys to Understanding

Subjects and Predicates

A sentence is made of two parts: a subject and a predicate.

A subject

is a noun or pronoun and the words that modify it.	A lot of Central High School sophomores like board games.
tells who or what the sentence is about.	My friends play them with their families.
can be about one person or thing.	Luis plays many board games.
can be about more than one person or thing.	Scrabble, chess, and checkers are his favorites.
can be short.	He is a sophomore.
can be long.	Luis, his parents, and all his cousins play board games on Sunday afternoons.

A predicate

is one or more verbs plus the rest of the sentence.	Ling is an actor. She sings and dances with her twin sister, Mai.
has a verb that tells what the subject is or does.	Ling and Mai play in the school band, too.
can be short.	They are talented.
can be long.	Ling can't decide between acting and playing music.

Circle the complete subject. Underline the complete predicate.

Example: (Their oldest brother) has an after-school job in the mall.

My father's favorite meal is chicken fried steak.

The complete subject is *My father's favorite meal*. The rest of the sentence is the complete predicate.

Avoid Fragments

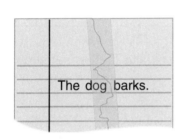

An incomplete sentence is also called a **sentence fragment**. It is a group of words that looks like a sentence but is not complete. It is missing a subject, a verb, or both. *Fragment* means a bit or broken piece.

Read this passage. The fragment is underlined.

> **Americans use a lot of water. <u>Over 100 gallons of water a day</u>.**

You can fix sentence fragments in two ways:

1. You can add the missing parts.

   This fragment is missing a subject and verb. You can make the fragment a complete sentence by adding a subject and a verb.

> **Americans use a lot of water. <u>The average American uses</u> over 100 gallons of water a day.**

2. You can combine the fragment with another sentence to make a new, complete sentence. (*Hint:* You might need to make changes to capitalization, punctuation, or grammar.)

> **The average American uses over 100 gallons of water a day.**

Check the best way to fix this fragment.

> **Instead of taking long baths, short showers.**

___ A. Instead of taking long baths, short showers and less hot water.

___ B. Instead of taking long baths, I take short showers to save water.

The fragment is missing a verb. A doesn't add the missing part. B fixes the fragment by adding a complete subject.

Practice A: Write *C* for a complete sentence. Write *F* for a fragment. Then fix the fragments.

<u>F</u> Barbecue chicken on the grill.<u>My dad likes barbecue chicken on the grill</u>.

____ 1.Dad starts the charcoal first. _____

____ 2.Lighter fluid on the charcoal. _____

____ 3.Makes the chicken taste bad. _____

____ 4 The grill has to be. _____

____ 5.He cooks each side about 20 minutes. _____

____ 6. Isn't cooked enough. _____

Practice B: Underline the fragments. Copy the paragraph in your notebook and fix the fragments.

Cherry Blossom Time

Japan has a flower festival every spring. Famous all over the world. It is the Cherry Blossom Festival. The flower of the cherry tree. It is the most popular flower in Japan. It blooms in the spring. Picnics and have special parties to see the flowers.

Practice C: In your notebook, write a statement, a question, and an exclamation about your favorite holiday or time of year. Check for subject–verb agreement, spelling, capitalization, and punctuation. Make sure there are no fragments.

My favorite time of year is spring when all the snow is gone.

What do I like about it?

I don't have to shovel another sidewalk until next winter!

SEE PAGE 199 FOR ANSWERS AND EXPLANATIONS.

Vary Sentence Types

Recognize Simple and Compound Sentences

Good writers include different sentence types in their writing to make it more interesting.

A simple sentence has a subject, a verb, and end punctuation. It is a complete thought. A simple sentence is also called an independent clause.

A simple sentence can be short or long. It can have one subject and one verb. It can also have more than one subject or more than one verb.

The Miami area has many nice beaches.
subject   verb

Miami Beach, Crandon Park Beach, and Mattheson Hammock are great beaches.
subject   verb

People swim, surf, and fish there.
verbs

A compound sentence is one way to combine ideas. A compound sentence has two independent clauses (simple sentences) joined by a **comma** + **and, but, for, nor, or, so,** or **yet**. These seven small words are called coordinating conjunctions.

The water at Crandon Park Beach is calm, for a sandbar protects the beach.

comma   coordinating conjunction

Write S for a simple sentence. Write C for a compound sentence.

___ A. I like lots of fruit, but my favorite fruit is fresh oranges.

___ B. My best friend, Carmen, doesn't like any fruit at all.

A is a compound sentence. It has two independent clauses: *I eat lots of fruit* and *my favorite fruit is fresh oranges*. They are connected by a comma 1 *but*. B has only one subject (*friend*) and verb (*doesn't like*). It is a simple sentence.

Here are some more ways to combine ideas in sentences:

- Use a **semicolon** between two independent clauses. The ideas in the sentences need to be related.

  The Miami area has many nice beaches**;** Miami Beach, Crandon Park Beach, and Mattheson Hammock are great beaches.

- Use a **semicolon + a transition word or phrase + a comma** between the two independent clauses. **Transition words** are words or phrases that link ideas. Transition words are also called **connectors**.

  The Miami area has many nice beaches**; in fact,** Miami Beach, Crandon Park Beach, and Mattheson Hammock are all great beaches.

 # Keys to Understanding

To combine sentences, first decide how the sentences are related. Then pick the connectors that show that kind of relationship.

Coordinating Conjunctions/ Other Connectors	Examples
to add information	
and	Visitors like Miami Beach, **and** many of them like Crandon Park Beach.
also, in addition, in fact, moreover	Visitors like Miami Beach**; in addition,** many of them like Crandon Park Beach.
to show contrast	
but, yet	Miami Beach is very crowded, **yet** people love walking around there.
however, even so, on the other hand, instead, otherwise	Miami Beach is very crowded**; even so,** people love walking around there.
to show cause and effect	
for, so	The midday sun is strong, **so** it's important to wear sun block.
therefore, consequently, as a result	The midday sun is strong**; therefore** it's important to wear sun block.
to show choices	
or	Children can swim at Crandon Park Beach, **or** they can collect seashells.
on the other hand, otherwise	Children can swim at Crandon Park Beach**; otherwise,** they can collect seashells
to compare ideas	
similarly, likewise	An evening barbecue is fun**; likewise,** everyone loves to make sundaes for dessert.

Strategies for Test-Taking Success: Writing © Heinle, Cengage Learning. Photocopying this page is prohibited by law.

Punctuate the sentence.

Doctors expect a bad flu season this year; consequently, they want everyone to get a flu shot.

Many people get high fever, body aches, and chills on the other hand some people have very mild symptoms.

Put a semicolon after chills *and a comma after* hand.

Avoid Run-on Sentences

A run-on sentence is two sentences joined together without a connector, punctuation, or both.

Missing the connector:

Miami Beach, Crandon Park Beach, and Mattheson Hammock are great beaches; people swim, surf, and fish there.

Missing punctuation:

Miami Beach, Crandon Park Beach, and Mattheson Hammock are great beaches so people swim, surf, and fish there.

Missing both:

Miami Beach, Crandon Park Beach, and Mattheson Hammock are great beaches people swim, surf, and fish there.

Correct:

Miami Beach, Crandon Park Beach, and Mattheson Hammock are great beaches, so people swim, surf, and fish there.

or

Miami Beach, Crandon Park Beach, and Mattheson Hammock are great beaches; people swim, surf, and fish there.

Write *MP* for missing punctuation. Write *MC* for missing connector. Write *MB* for missing both.

____ A. Volleyball is a great activity at Crandon Park Beach but some kids like to play paddle ball.

____ B. You need five or six people to play volleyball you need only two people to play paddle ball.

____ C. Volleyball is always popular, sometimes it's hard to find an empty court.

A. MP; B. MB; C. MC

Strategy 13 Vary Sentence Types   **75**

Practice A: Choose a connector to combine and rewrite the sentences in your notebook. Change capitalization and punctuation as needed.

(but / in fact) The U.S. Supreme Court starts working on the first Monday in October. It doesn't have a special ending date.

The U.S. Supreme Court starts working on the first Monday in October, but it doesn't have a fixed ending date.

1. (so / furthermore) Nine justices, or judges, are on the Supreme Court. Each justice will serve for the rest of his or her life.

2. (for / however) The president picks judges for the Supreme Court. The Senate can accept or reject the president's choices.

3. (yet / otherwise) The Court gets about 5,000 requests to hear cases each year. The justices hear only about 200 of them.

4. (or / in addition) Each side sends written statements to the Court. One lawyer from each side has 30 minutes to speak and answer questions.

5. (and / instead) All nine justices discuss and vote on each case. A simple majority of five justices decides the case.

Practice B: Complete the sentences below with your own ideas. Write in your notebook. Add punctuation as needed. Check that you don't have any run-on sentences.

At age 8, I fell in love with science, and *I want to be a biologist some day.*

1. The evening news is interesting to watch in fact. . .

2. My family wants me to go into business however. . .

3. Teenagers can be responsible for making good choices so. . .

4. I have to get my bike fixed therefore. . .

SEE PAGE 199 FOR ANSWERS AND EXPLANATIONS.

Strategies for Test-Taking Success: Writing © Heinle, Cengage Learning. Photocopying this page is prohibited by law.

Complex Sentences

A **complex sentence** is an independent clause + a dependent clause. A dependent clause has a subject and a verb. But a dependent clause is *not a complete thought* because it begins with a connector. A dependent clause by itself is a fragment.

Examples of dependent clauses:

- although you read them all the time

- as you write your essay

To make a dependent clause a complete sentence, connect it to an independent clause. Together, they make a complete complex sentence.

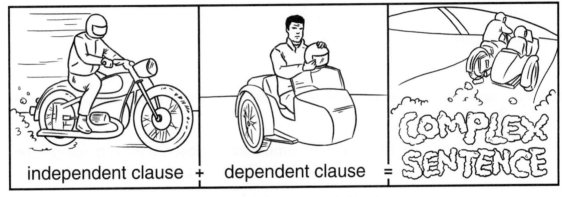

independent clause + dependent clause = COMPLEX SENTENCE

Sometimes it's hard to write a dependent clause <u>although you read them all the time.</u>

Use dependent clauses to vary your sentences <u>as you write your essay.</u>

The order of the clauses in a complex sentence is usually not important. Either sentence can be written first.

independent clause + dependent clause

You don't need a comma (when) the independent clause is first.

independent clause   connector   dependent clause

OR

dependent clause + comma + independent clause

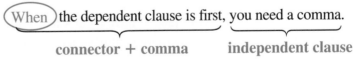

(When) the dependent clause is first, you need a comma.

connector + comma   independent clause

Keys to Understanding

Connectors for Complex Sentences

to give reasons	
because, since, so that	Since I have a bus pass, I won't have to walk.
to contrast ideas	
although, even though, despite	It was sunny today even though the forecast was for rain.
to show time order	
before, after, until, while, as, when, whenever	Until the temperature in the north warms up, birds stay in the south.
to show conditions	
if, unless, whether	You need calcium if you want strong teeth and bones.
to show result or effect	
so that	Please hang up the towel so that it dries faster.

Write *S* for the simple sentence, *CD* for the compound sentence, and *CX* for the complex sentence.

___ A. We leave for school at 7:45, and we arrive by 8:10.

___ B. Teachers get to school before the students get off the buses.

___ C. The teachers and students meet during homeroom.

A. CD. Two independent clauses are joined by a comma + *and*. B. CX. The independent clause is *Teachers get to school early*, and the dependent clause is *before the students get off the buses*. C. S. The subject is *The teachers and students* and the complete predicate is *meet during a 15-minute homeroom*.

Practice A: Underline the independent clause once and the dependent clause twice. Circle the connectors in the complex sentences.

(Even though) most people like to shop in malls, not everything about a shopping mall is enjoyable.

1. You have to have a car since you can't walk to a suburban mall.
2. While there is always a big parking lot, there are usually few trees to shade your car in summer.
3. You will see some of the same stores if you shop in malls across the country.

Practice B: Choose the correct connector. Combine and rewrite each pair of sentences into a complex sentence. Change capitalization or punctuation as needed.

(when / despite) My family goes food shopping on Friday night. We like to have a plan.

When my family goes food shopping on Friday night, we like to have a plan.

1. (before / because) I'm in charge of canned goods and paper products. I can bend down low to check out the bottom shelf.

   _____

   _____

2. (since / whether) My sister loves milk and cheese. She is responsible for dairy products.

   _____

   _____

3. (whenever / unless) Mom and Dad decide to cook fish, meat, or chicken. We will have an all-vegetable meal.

   _____

   _____

4. (until / so that) I didn't want an all-vegetable meal. I tasted my parents' great vegetarian rice and pasta dishes.

   _____

   _____

5. (even though / so that) I don't like to shop. Our plan makes it fast and easy.

   _____

   _____

Practice C: Write five complex sentences in your notebook. Use a different connector in each sentence.

> **Topic:** Describe an activity you do with your friends or family.

My friends and I go sledding while the snow is still falling.

SEE PAGE 200 FOR ANSWERS AND EXPLANATIONS.

Make Your Sentences Interesting

Good writing includes good details. Here are three ways to add details to your sentences:

1. **Combine separate ideas into a series.** It's not interesting to read sentences that all have the same structure. It's boring to read sentences where words or phrases are repeated.

   I like bananas. I like pears, too. I eat a lot of mangoes.

   These sentences are too similar. They are all short. Words are repeated. All the details are about fruit. To fix the problem, put the details into a series. (Remember to separate items in a series with commas.)

   I like bananas, pears, and mangoes.

2. **Combine related ideas into one sentence.** You can combine similar ideas in one sentence instead of putting each idea in its own sentence.

   A roller coaster is fast. It is an amusement park ride. It is scary.

   A roller-coaster is a fast and scary amusement park ride.

3. **Insert details into sentences.** You can insert details or extra information into a sentence. Put commas around the extra details.

   Abraham Lincoln was born in Illinois. He was the 16th president.

   Abraham Lincoln, the 16th president, was born in Illinois.

Strategies for Test-Taking Success: Writing © Heinle, Cengage Learning. Photocopying this page is prohibited by law.

You can insert details with *who, which,* and *that.*

- Use *who* to add details about a person.

Marco's father is wearing a blue suit. He is at the front of the line.

Marco's father, who is wearing a blue suit, is at the front of the line.

- Use *which* to add details about a thing.

Thanksgiving Day falls on the 28th this year. It is always on the last Thursday in November.

Thanksgiving Day, which is always on the last Thursday in November, falls on the 28th this year.

- Use *that* to add details about a person or a thing.

The person that gets the job is very lucky.

The dull movie that won an Oscar last year is on television.

Check the sentence that is correct.

___ A. Ming, which is happy, moved to a new house.

___ B. Her new house, which is closer to school, is comfortable.

B is correct because *which* is used for things, not people.

Practice A: Combine each group of sentences into one sentence. Add or change words, punctuation, and capitalization as needed.

My father is a mechanic. He is great at his job.

My father, a mechanic, is great at his job.

1. He works at an auto repair shop. It is far from our home.

    _____

    _____

2. Mr. Kendal owns the shop. He trusts my father with all the cars.

    _____

    _____

3. My father can fix sedans and sports cars. He can fix vans. He can even fix trucks.

    _____

    _____

4. My father wants his own shop. He needs to work closer to home.

    _____

    _____

5. He already has a name for his new shop. It is Ng's First-Rate Repairs.

    _____

    _____

Practice B: Write four sentences in your notebook. In each sentence, use either a series, a combination of similar ideas, or *who* or *which*.

> **Topic:** Write about the job of a parent or adult you admire.

Mr. Gonzalez, my neighbor, is a social worker.

SEE PAGE 200 FOR ANSWERS AND EXPLANATIONS.

Strategies for Test-Taking Success: Writing © Heinle, Cengage Learning. Photocopying this page is prohibited by law.

Use Parallel Structure

A sentence with **parallel structure** uses the *same forms and the same parts of speech* for all the details in the sentence.

 Keys to Understanding

If your details describe something, make them *all* adjectives.

> **Not parallel:** Tomás is tall, smart, and <u>says funny things</u>.
> **Parallel:** Tomás is <u>tall, smart, and funny</u>.

If your details tell what someone or something does, make them all verbs. Use the *same verb form* and *tense* for all of them.

> **Not parallel:** Malina likes <u>playing soccer and to swim</u>.
>
> **Parallel:** Malina likes playing soccer and <u>swimming</u>.
>
> or
>
> **Parallel:** Malina likes <u>to play soccer</u> and to swim.

Don't mix words or phrases with clauses.

> **Not parallel:** Our class trip was to Philadelphia, Gettysburg, and <u>we went to Washington, D.C.</u>
>
> **Parallel:** Our class trip was <u>to Philadelphia, Gettysburg, and Washington D.C.</u>

Check the sentence with parallel structure.

___ A. The best teachers have a sense of humor, are grading papers fairly, and really like kids.

___ B. The best teachers have a sense of humor, grade papers fairly, and really like kids.

> You are correct if you checked B. A does not have parallel verb forms. It uses the simple present (*have, have*) and the present continuous (*are grading*).

Practice A: Underline the part of the sentence that is not parallel. Rewrite the sentence using parallel structure.

You can get calcium from milk, cheese, and <u>eating yogurt</u>.

<u>You can get calcium from milk, cheese, and yogurt.</u>

1. Han spends Saturdays emailing friends or to watch a movie.

   _____

   _____

2. When you ride your bike, always wear a helmet and you have to follow the rules of the road.

   _____

   _____

3. Put cocoa and sugar into the cup, pour in hot milk, and you need to stir until the milk turns dark brown.

   _____

   _____

4. Fredo likes Best Boots because they are comfortable, sturdy, and they are inexpensive.

   _____

   _____

5. Mr. Michaels was a soldier, a teacher, and worked as a reporter.

   _____

   _____

Practice B: Underline the problems with parallel structure in this paragraph. Then rewrite the paragraph correctly in your notebook.

The Caribbean: Then and Now

When Christopher Columbus first arrived in the Caribbean, he found three tribes: the Arawak, the Carib, and a tribe called the Ciboney. The Caribbean includes over 100 islands, and there are 20 countries today. The climate in the Caribbean is warm and also considered tropical. Tourists come in the winter months to get away from the cold weather, to lie on the beautiful beaches, and go swimming around the coral reefs. Tourists also like to snorkel, to fish, and go sailing.

SEE PAGE 200 FOR ANSWERS AND EXPLANATIONS.

CHAPTER 4: REVIEW TEST

Mark your answers on the Answer Grid.

Read this story. Then answer Questions 1 through 9. There are errors in the story. You will answer questions about the errors.

Chocolate Chip Cookies

(1)   I love chocolate chip cookies. My parents make them for me. I get them at the bakery and the supermarket. I buy them at school. I wanted to know how to make them myself. I asked my cousin for her favorite recipe. I call the recipe "Mimi's Best Chocolate Chip Cookies."

2 sticks butter	2 cups flour
¾ cup white sugar	1 tsp. baking soda
1 cup brown sugar	1 tsp. salt
2 eggs	1½ cups semisweet chocolate chips
1 tsp. vanilla	

(2)   Preheat the oven to 350 degrees Fahrenheit. Mix the butter and sugar together with a wooden spoon. Mix in the eggs. Mix in the vanilla. Sprinkle the flour, baking soda, and salt into the batter; and continue to mix. Add the chocolate chips.

(3)   Wash your hands form lumps of dough with your fingers or a spoon. Put them on buttered cookie sheets. Because they will spread. Make sure there's enough space between the lumps. Put the cookies in the oven. For eight to ten minutes. Let the cookies cool for five minutes. Then carefully slide them off the cookie sheet with a spatula put them on a wire rack to cool some more.

(4)   Now I know how to make delicious cookies whenever I want. I don't need my parents to make them, or go to the bakery or supermarket, or buy them at school. There's only one problem. Now that I know how to make cookies, no one wants me to stop. They ask me to make cookies all the time! I just give them the recipe. They can make the cookies themselves.

1 **What is the BEST way to combine these sentences from paragraph 1?**

> My parents make them for me. I get them at the bakery and the supermarket. I buy them at school.

A My parents make them for me, get them at the bakery and the supermarket, or buy them at school.

B My parents make them for me. I also get them at the bakery, the supermarket, and I buy them at school.

C My parents make them for me, or I buy them at the bakery, at the supermarket, or at school.

D My parents make them for me; so, I get them at the bakery and the supermarket; and then, I get them at school.

GO ON

2 What is the BEST way to combine these sentences from paragraph 1?

> I asked my cousin for her favorite recipe. I call the recipe "Mimi's Best Chocolate Chip Cookies."

A I asked my cousin for her favorite recipe, which I call "Mimi's Best Chocolate Chip Cookies."

B I asked my cousin for her favorite recipe, who I call "Mimi's Best Chocolate Chip Cookies."

C I asked my cousin for her favorite recipe, I call the recipe "Mimi's Best Chocolate Chip Cookies."

D I asked my cousin for her favorite recipe even though I call the recipe "Mimi's Best Chocolate Chip Cookies."

3 What is the BEST way to rewrite these sentences from paragraph 2?

> Mix in the eggs. Mix in the vanilla.

A Mix in the eggs, or mix in the vanilla.

B Mix in the eggs and the vanilla.

C Mix in the eggs; therefore, mix in the vanilla.

D Mix in the eggs, mix in the vanilla.

4 What is the BEST way to rewrite this sentence from paragraph 2?

> Sprinkle the flour, baking soda, and salt into the batter; and continue to mix.

A Sprinkle the flour, baking soda, and salt into the batter as you continue to mix.

B Sprinkle the flour, baking soda, and salt into the batter, continue to mix.

C Sprinkle the flour, baking soda, and salt into the batter continue to mix.

D Make no change.

5 What change, if any, should be made to this sentence from paragraph 3?

> Wash your hands form lumps of dough with your fingers or a spoon.

A Change *your* to *you're*.

B Insert a semicolon after *hands*.

C Insert *using* after *or*.

D Make no change.

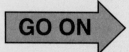
GO ON

6 What is the BEST way to combine these sentences from paragraph 3?

> Because they will spread. Make sure there's enough space between the lumps.

A Because they will spread; consequently, make sure there's enough space between the lumps.

B Because they will spread; make sure there's enough space between the lumps.

C Because they will spread make sure there's enough space between the lumps.

D Because they will spread, make sure there's enough space between the lumps.

7 What is the BEST way to revise these sentences from paragraph 3?

> Put the cookies in the oven. For eight to ten minutes. Let the cookies cool for five minutes.

A Put the cookies in the oven for eight to ten minutes let the cookies cool for five minutes.

B Put the cookies in the oven. For eight to ten minutes let the cookies cool. For five minutes.

C Put the cookies in the oven. For eight to ten minutes; in addition, let the cookies cool for five minutes.

D Put the cookies in the oven for eight to ten minutes. Let the cookies cool for five minutes.

8 What change, if any, should be made to this sentence from paragraph 3?

> Then carefully slide them off the cookie sheet with a spatula put them on a wire rack to cool some more.

A Change *carefully* to *careful.*

B Insert a comma after *spatula.*

C Change *spatula put* to *spatula. Put.*

D Make no change.

 9 Look at these sentences from paragraph 4. Write a compound sentence that combines these sentences.

I just give them the recipe. They can make the cookies themselves.

_____

_____

_____

 GO ON

Read this paragraph. Then answer Questions 10 through 13.

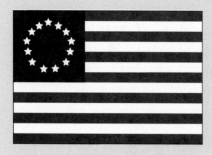

(1) Francis Hopkinson designed the first American flag. (2) He signed the Declaration of Independence, too. (3) Because he wanted the flag to be ready for the new nation, Hopkinson started working early. (4) The design included 13 stars and 13 stripes to represent the original 13 states. (5) Today the flag still has 13 stripes although now there are 50 stars to represent the current number of states. (6) The colors red, white, and blue also have special meanings. (7) Red stands for strength and courage, white for purity and innocence, and justice and patience are symbolized by blue.

10 What is the BEST way to combine sentences 1 and 2?

A Francis Hopkinson designed the first American flag; however, he signed the Declaration of Independence, too.

B Francis Hopkinson designed the first American flag, he signed the Declaration of Independence.

C Francis Hopkinson designed the first American flag he signed the Declaration of Independence.

D Francis Hopkinson, who signed the Declaration of Independence, designed the first American flag.

11 Look at sentence 3. It is a complex sentence with one independent clause and one dependent clause. Write two simple sentences that express the same idea as the complex one.

_____

_____

_____

12 Choose the BEST word for the underlined part of sentence 5.

> Today the flag still has 13 stripes <u>although</u> now there are 50 stars to represent the current number of states.

A although

B because

C unless

D whether

13 How should the underlined part of sentence 7 be rewritten to create parallel structure?

> Red stands for strength and courage, white for purity and innocence, <u>and justice and patience are symbolized by blue</u>.

A people say blue stands for justice and patience

B justice and patience means blue

C blue for justice and patience

D Make no change.

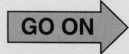

Write your answers to Items 14 through 16 on the lines.

14 Look at these sentences. Combine them with a semicolon and a connector. Change words and punctuation as needed.

Hopkinson represented New Jersey. Hopkinson was born in Pennsylvania.

_____

_____

15 Look at these sentences. Write one sentence that combines them.

Betsy Ross did not sew the nation's first flag. She is an American legend.

_____

_____

16 Look at these sentences. Write one complex sentence that combines these sentences.

Hopkinson complained to the government. Hopkinson wasn't paid for his work.

_____

_____

STOP. THIS IS THE END OF THE REVIEW TEST.
SEE PAGE 201 FOR ANSWERS AND EXPLANATIONS.

Chapter 5

Write Paragraphs

Think about the Main Idea

Identify the Main Idea

TIP

A *title* or *headline* often tells you the main idea of a book or an article.

Title: *Strategies for Test-Taking Success*

Headline: "East City Soccer Team Beats Midland, 3–2"

A paragraph is a group of sentences about one main idea. It is the most important idea in a paragraph. Sometimes the main idea is called the *main point* or the *central idea*.

Use a topic sentence to express the main idea.

Three kinds of topic sentences in paragraphs are:

- A general statement: *The Statue of Liberty is a famous attraction in New York City.*

- A question: *Where do most tourists go in New York City?*

- An opinion: *I think the Statue of Liberty is the most interesting place to visit in New York City.*

Write *G* for general statement. Write *O* for opinion.

____ A. Teens use the Internet for sending e-mails, chatting online, and getting homework help.

TIP

The people who read your writing will be looking for the main idea. Make it easy for them: *Start* your paragraph with a topic sentence.

____ B. The author picked a great title for her article.

A is a general statement. B is an opinion.

Practice A: Read the paragraphs below. Then check the best topic sentence for each paragraph.

1.   The Underground Railroad wasn't underground, and it wasn't a railroad. In fact, the Underground Railroad wasn't a train at all. It was a series of secret houses, tunnels, and roads. Tubman used it to run away from a Maryland slave owner. She hid from slave catchers who wanted to take her back to her owner or even kill her. After many months, Tubman crossed into Pennsylvania, where slavery was illegal. She was free at last. She spent the rest of her life helping other slaves escape to freedom on the Underground Railroad.

    ___ A. Slave catchers were a great danger to slaves who were escaping.

    ___ B. In large cities, there are underground trains called subways.

    ___ C. Harriet Tubman escaped from slavery on the Underground Railroad.

2.   In 1889, the first home delivery of food was made in Italy. Vendors carried pizzas in large boxes on their heads. They sold pizzas to hungry people on the streets. Soon, women opened windows and called out for pizzas. The vendors passed pizzas through the windows, creating the first home delivery of food.

    ___ A. Calling out for fast food is still popular today.

    ___ B. Did you know that people ordered take-out meals more than 100 years ago?

    ___ C. The first pizzas were made in Greece.

Practice B: Write a topic sentence for this paragraph.

    East coast black bears are usually shy and gentle. They don't like to fight. They run away instead. Black bears are vegetarians, too. They eat roots, nuts, and berries. They need a lot of space that is safe and quiet. They like to live far from towns, highways, and people.

_____

_____

_____

SEE PAGE 202 FOR ANSWERS AND EXPLANATIONS.

Strategies for Test-Taking Success: Writing © Heinle, Cengage Learning. Photocopying this page is prohibited by law.

Add Supporting Details

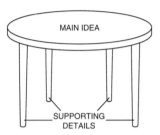

MAIN IDEA

SUPPORTING
DETAILS

A good paragraph needs more than a good topic sentence. It also needs supporting details so your reader can understand your main idea. Supporting details are general information, facts, and examples.

Keys to Understanding

A paragraph has one main idea. The topic sentence expresses the main idea. A paragraph also has several supporting details.

Topic sentence: A gorilla eats many plants, but it isn't a vegetarian.

General Information	Facts	Examples
It eats leaves, fruit, and tree bark.	Leaves supply protein. Fruit supplies sugars. Bark supplies fiber.	A gorilla will also eat ants or worms.

Here's one way to combine the topic sentence and supporting details into a paragraph.

A gorilla eats many plants, but it isn't a vegetarian. Its diet is mainly leaves, fruit, and tree bark. Leaves supply protein, fruit supplies sugars, and bark supplies fiber. However, plants aren't the gorilla's only food. For example, sometimes a gorilla likes to snack on tasty ants or worms.

Another way to support the main idea is to give reasons. Reasons answer the question *Why?*

Strategies for Test-Taking Success: Writing © Heinle, Cengage Learning. Photocopying this page is prohibited by law.

TIP

Connectors that show reasons:

because / so

since / so that

Keys to Understanding

Topic sentence: Mountain gorillas are an endangered species.

Question: **Why** *are mountain gorillas endangered?*

Reason 1	Reason 2	Reason 3
Hunters kill them for food or sport.	There is often war in their territory.	People chop down the trees gorillas eat.

Here's one way to combine the main idea and reasons into a paragraph.

Underline the connectors that show reasons.

> Mountain gorillas are an endangered species. There are three main reasons for this sad situation. First, few gorillas are left because hunters kill them for food or sport. Next, there is often war where they live, so some gorillas get shot. Last, gorillas have less food to eat since people chop down trees for fuel.

The connectors that show reasons are *because*, *so*, and *since*.

Practice A: Check the sentences that support this main idea. Then use the information to write a paragraph in your notebook. Change the sentences as needed.

> Native American science students planned an experiment that NASA astronauts carried out on the space shuttle.

EXAMPLE:

_✓_ The students compared how potatoes grow in natural soil and in man-made soil.

___ 1. French fried, boiled, and mashed are examples of good ways to cook potatoes.

___ 2. The man-made soil was like the red dirt found on Mars.

___ 3. The potato plant is a vine.

___ 4. The experiment was nicknamed "Spuds in Space" because astronauts did it in the space shuttle.

Practice B: Write three supporting details for each main idea below. Give details, facts, examples, or reasons.

1. A dog is truly a person's best friend.

   Dogs are always happy to see you. _____

   _____

   _____

2. You can learn important things from television.

   _____

   _____

   _____

3. My plans for the future are always changing.

   _____

   _____

   _____

SEE PAGE 202 FOR ANSWERS AND EXPLANATIONS.

Use Appropriate Tone, Language, and Word Choice

You Already Know Your Audience

When you write, you usually have to figure out who your audience is. When you take a writing test, you know who your audience is: the people who will grade your test.

You also need to be sure that your tone, language, and word choice match the purpose of your writing.

Tone

The tone says what you think or feel about a topic. Tone is your opinion about a subject. It shows in the words you choose. Your audience needs to know that you are *interested* in your subject.

Show *enthusiasm* in your writing. These are *your* ideas. Let the audience know that the ideas are *important* to you.

Compare the following paragraphs. The topic is the same: the writer's future career. Which one has a more interesting tone?

> ### It's Not Brain Surgery!
> #### by Artie Guy
>
> People who know me aren't surprised. At four, my twin brother was racing around the yard on his tricycle while I was inside with my finger paints. In middle school, the other kids ran around the soccer field, but not me. I drew pictures of them kicking goals. Now those kids are high school football players. I'm on the newspaper staff, and it's <u>my</u> cartoons that everyone enjoys. What's my future job? It's not brain surgery. I'm an artist, and I love it.

My Future Job
by Artless Plain

I always liked to draw. I am good at it. I liked finger painting in kindergarten. I drew pictures of my friends in middle school. Now that I'm in high school, I draw cartoons for the school paper. People think my cartoons are funny. I think I am a good artist. I think I will be an artist in the future.

Artie's and Artless's paragraphs have the same main idea and similar details. But the tone of the paragraphs is very different.

Artie starts with a funny title, "It's Not Brain Surgery!" He uses strong verbs and colorful examples that you can "see." You can also tell that Artie enjoys writing about the subject. That makes it easier for his audience to enjoy reading about it. His tone is upbeat, positive, and lively (*it's my cartoons that everyone enjoys*).

"My Future Job" isn't a very exciting title. Artless repeats words and phrases, and she writes only simple sentences. Artless's paragraph isn't bad, but the tone is plain and dull (*drew–draw, People think–I think*). Her audience probably won't get excited about the paragraph, and her score may not be as good as Artie's.

Language

Language is the words you use in your writing. Use language that fits your subject and holds your audience's attention.

Use standard English when you write. Standard English is understood by most English speakers.

- Standard English does *not* use slang. (Slang is only understood by *some* English speakers.)

    Slang: I <u>ain't gonna</u> write <u>no junk</u>.

    Standard: I'm not going to write badly.

- Standard English does *not* repeat unnecessary words.

    Repeated Words: The Mojave <u>Desert</u> is a <u>desert</u> in California, Arizona, and Nevada.

    Standard: The Mojave Desert is located in California, Arizona, and Nevada.

- Standard language does *not* use Internet shorthand or text-messaging language.

Internet shorthand: <u>BTW</u>, <u>R U</u> finished with the test?

Standard: By the way, are you finished with the test?

Word Choice

Good writers pick their words with great care. They use precise[1] words to say what they mean. Good writers also don't use words that are too general or overused.

Too general: The water is kind of hot.

Precise: The water is boiling.

The phrase *kind of hot* is too general. The water could be sitting in the sun or over heat.

The verb *boil* is exact. You can tell that the water is bubbling over heat, and that it is 212° F (100° C).

Overused: Our trip was nice.

Precise: Our trip was enjoyable.

The word *nice* is often overused. It's hard to know what happened on a "nice trip."

The word *enjoyable* is more precise. It tells you that the trip was fun.

Use synonyms to avoid overused words. Use a dictionary or thesaurus to find more synonyms.

Overused Word	A Synonym	My Synonyms
a lot	plenty of	many
big	huge	
good	fine	
interesting	remarkable	
nice	pleasant	
pretty	good-looking	

[1] **precise**: accurate, exact, correct

Practice A: Write *S* for standard language. Write *I* for slang or Internet shorthand. Write *R* for repeated words. Rewrite the sentences you marked with *S*, *I*, or *R*. Write your sentences in your notebook.

EXAMPLE:

___I___ So here's how I scope it out.

This is what I think.

___ 1. Yo! Whazzup?

___ 2. Vary your sentences to keep your audience's interest.

___ 3. The senator disagrees with the committee; therefore, he won't vote for the bill.

___ 4. The planet Pluto is called a planet, but it may not be one.

___ 5. B @ yr place @ 6.

___ 6. Savings bonds are bonds that are tax free if you use them for college tuition.

Practice B: Revise this paragraph in your notebook. Use a more precise word for each underlined word. Use a synonym from the box or one of your own.

above	believe	connected	higher	low	traveled

believe

    Scientists <u>feel</u> that the first people in California were from Asia. People (1) <u>walked</u> to North America from Asia across a land bridge. This was land that (2) <u>hooked up</u> the two continents. People and animals crossed the land bridge from Asia to North America when the ocean was (3) <u>low down</u>. At that time, the land bridge was (4) <u>on top of</u> the water's surface. Today, the level of the ocean is (5) <u>up</u> and the land bridge is below the surface.

Practice C: In your notebook, write a precise description for each sentence below.

My best friend is very friendly. She enjoys talking to everyone at school, whether she's known them for years or just introduced herself to them.

1. Our school is a big building.

2. Cafeteria food is good.

3. That is a nice sweater.

SEE PAGE 202 FOR ANSWERS AND EXPLANATIONS.

Strategy 18   Use Appropriate Tone, Language, and Word Choice   **99**

Use Transitions

In Chapter 4, you learned about coordinating conjunctions and other connectors. These connectors are also used as transitions.

A transition means a change or movement.

When you write a paragraph, transitions[2] help the audience understand the move from:

- the main idea to a supporting detail

   I agree with the school ban on junk food for three reasons. First of all, it's easier for us to use what we learn in health class about eating good food.

- one idea in a paragraph to the next idea

   I agree with the school ban on junk food for three reasons. First of all, it's easier for us to use what we learn in health class about eating good food. For example, it's easier to choose an apple for dessert if there aren't any cookies in the cafeteria.

[2] You will learn how to use transitions between paragraphs in Chapter 6, "Write Essays."

Here are some transition[3] words and phrases and the relationships to supporting details they show.

Keys to Understanding

Relationship	Transition Words
Sequences	first . . . second . . . third . . . , first of all, then, next, last, finally
Time	after, earlier, from then on, later, long ago, in the past, so far, soon, then
Compare	by the same token, on the one hand, despite
Contrast	in contrast to, regardless, still, on the other hand
Examples	even, for example, for instance, for one thing, in fact, of course, such as

Check the sentence with the transition that fits the idea.

___ A. It's true that the best things in life are free. For instance, people need a home, food, and clothing.

___ B. It's true that the best things in life are free. For instance, conversations with friends don't cost money and are very rewarding.

The sentences in A show contrast, but *For instance* isn't a contrasting transition. B is correct. Its sentences are a statement and an example. Use *for instance* as a transition for examples.

[3] You can review other transitions on pages 74 and 78.

Practice A: Choose a transition word or phrase that fits the ideas.

I think Emperor penguins are the best fathers in the animal world.

_____*After*_____ the mother penguin lays her egg, she leaves it to find
  (After / Next)
food. (1)_____, the father stays with the egg and protects it.
    (From then on / By the same token)
He balances the egg on his feet for months. (2)_____
                                        (In fact, / Regardless)
he doesn't eat the whole time because the egg might freeze if he

leaves it. (3)_____ the wind and cold, he doesn't let go of the
      (Despite / Finally)
egg until the female comes back with food. (4)_____ many
                                      (Finally / In contrast to)
others in the animal kingdom, the Emperor penguin is a fearless and

loving father.

Practice B: In your notebook, write a paragraph with directions for
one of the topics below. Be sure to include transition words or
phrases.

> **Topic 1.** How to Make My Favorite Lunch
>
> **Topic 2.** How to Ride a Skateboard
>
> **Topic 3.** How to Find Your Homework Assignment Online

*It's easy to make a delicious peanut butter and banana
sandwich. First, put all the ingredients on the table. Next . . .*

SEE PAGE 203 FOR ANSWERS AND EXPLANATIONS.

Paragraph Unity

Paragraph unity means that:

- all the sentences belong in the paragraph

- no sentences are missing

- the sentences are in order, with a clear beginning, middle, and end

The paragraph is about one topic. Each detail should contribute to the main idea.

Make sure that no important details are missing from the paragraph.

Make sure the sentences are in order.

Look at the word web below. Cross out the detail that doesn't belong.

All the details belong except *mine is free*, which is about the cost of e-mail, not ways to use it.

Practice A: Read the paragraph below. Underline the two sentences that are out of order. Think about where the two sentences go. Then rewrite the paragraph correctly in your notebook.

(1) For years, the only way to get across San Francisco Bay was by boat. (2) Most people believed no one could build a bridge across the bay. (3) They said that a mile was too long for a bridge. (4) He never gave up. (5) The fog was too thick, the winds were too strong, and the ocean currents were deadly. (6) One engineer and bridge builder named Joseph Strauss made it happen. (7) Finally, in 1937, the beautiful Golden Gate Bridge opened, reaching more than a mile from San Francisco to Marin County. (8) Yet the bridge got built.

Practice B: Read the paragraph below.

1. Cross out the sentence that doesn't belong.

2. Then, check the detail from the list following the paragraph that can be added to this paragraph.

Everyone wins with solar roofs. That's what supporters say. People get cleaner air and energy independence. Others say the extra tax is unfair. Home owners will get money back when they install a solar system. The new law even gives extra money for solar energy in public housing.

___ A. Clean energy will increase from 100 to more than 3,000 megawatts a year.

___ B. Some people think solar roofs will cost too much.

___ C. In contrast, opponents of solar roofs say the bill has many problems.

SEE PAGE 203 FOR ANSWERS AND EXPLANATIONS.

Write Single and Multiple Paragraph Essays

Your writing can have one paragraph or several paragraphs. Each paragraph can have only *one* main idea and topic sentence.

Write a Single-Paragraph Essay

TIP

Don't forget to indent the first line of every paragraph.

Sometimes you will write one paragraph about a topic. This kind of paragraph states the main idea in the topic sentence, gives two or three details, and ends with a summary sentence.

Reread "It's Not Brain Surgery!" on page 96 for an example of a single-paragraph essay.

Write a Multiple-Paragraph Essay

You often have to write essays three to five paragraphs long. A graphic organizer can help you organize your ideas for a longer piece of writing.

Title	The Witch in the Woods
Beginning: Introduce topic, characters, setting	Once upon a time, a woodcutter lived in the woods with his children.
Middle: Describe events or problems	First, a mean, old witch trapped the children in her house. Then, she tried to fatten them up because she wanted to eat them.
End: Review events or resolve the problem	The children killed the witch and found their way home. Their father was very happy, and the little family lived happily ever after.

Title	Why I'm Voting for Maria for Treasurer by Paolo Cruz
Beginning/Introduction: State your main idea and preview supporting details	I'm supporting Maria for treasurer, and I think you should support her, too. She has great ideas, gets people involved, and has lots of energy.
Middle/Body: Two to three complete paragraphs with supporting details	Last year Maria came up with the idea for a *Run for Your Heart* . . . So that everyone participated, Maria made sure . . . Even though everyone else stopped, Maria kept on . . .
End/Conclusion: A summary of the main points	In conclusion, I think you should join me and vote for Maria for treasurer. That is, if you think the job needs someone with great ideas, strong people skills, and endless energy.

Where would you find each of these sentences in an essay? Write *I* for introduction. Write *B* for body. Write *C* for conclusion.

___ 1. Anyone can see that the trip takes longer every day.

___ 2. Public transportation is a major problem in the city.

___ 3. In short, it's up to Congress to improve the buses and trains.

1. B; 2. I; 3. C

Practice: Read the paragraphs below. Decide whether they are in the *introduction, body,* or *conclusion* of an essay.

After we unloaded the boat, we put up a tent and made beds of dried grass. Then we set out to explore.[4] *body*

1. But according to the laws of Alabama, Rosa Parks had to give her seat to a white man. She worked hard all day, and she was tired. She decided to keep her seat. Her decision changed her life—and the country—forever. _____

2. My first memories are of a large, rolling meadow with a small pond. As a colt, I was too young to eat grass, so I lived on my mother's milk.[5] _____

3. In summary, these small, controlled fires clear away old, dead trees and brush. Controlled fires are a good way to protect young, healthy forests. _____

4. A new study shows that about 17 million students use the Internet. These middle and high schoolers think the Internet improves their schoolwork. They think it improves their social life, too. _____

SEE PAGE 203 FOR ANSWERS AND EXPLANATIONS.

[4] Adapted from *The Swiss Family Robinson* by Johann Wyss.
[5] Adapted from *Black Beauty* by Anna Sewell.

CHAPTER 5: REVIEW TEST

Mark the answers to these questions on the Answer Grid.

Corey made the Writing Plan below to organize her ideas. Read her plan to answer Questions 1 through 3.

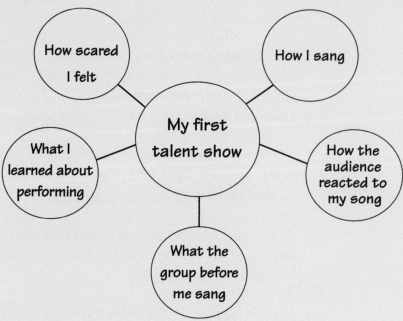

1 Which idea should be crossed off Corey's Writing Plan?

   A. How I sang

   B. How the audience reacted to my song

   C. What the group before me sang

   D. What I learned about performing

2 Based on the information in Corey's Writing Plan, which idea can be added to the plan?

   A. What song I sang

   B. Other places I sang

   C. I sing in the school chorus

   D. My second talent show

3 Based on the information in Corey's Writing Plan, what kind of paper is she planning to write?

   A. a paper that tells a story about a famous singer

   B. a paper that describes her favorite kind of music

   C. a paper that lists interview questions

   D. a paper that explains what her first talent show was like

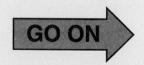

A Change My School Needs

(1) One thing I would like to see more of at my school is healthy food. (2) Oh, I'll admit it. (3) I love cookies and chips as much as the next kid. (4) I know I can't live on junk food alone. (5) My mother has diabetes, and my dad has heart problems. (6) Chocolate is delicious but unhealthy. (7) I often go with them to see the doc. (8) The one thing we hear over and over is: "Change your diet." (9) It would be great for my school to support better eating habits.

4 Which transition should be added to the beginning of sentence 4 to help connect the ideas in the paragraph?

   A. Also,

   B. Such as,

   C. However,

   D. Finally,

5 How should sentence 7 be rewritten for precision of word choice?

   A. I often go with them to their medical slot.

   B. I often go with them to their doctor meeting.

   C. I often go with them to their medical appointments.

   D. Make no change.

6 What sentence does NOT belong in this essay?

   A. Sentence 4

   B. Sentence 5

   C. Sentence 6

   D. Sentence 7

7 Which sentence could BEST be added after sentence 8?

   A. Some doctors say exercise is even more important.

   B. Now we only have desserts on holidays.

   C. Less stress would help, too.

   D. My experience has taught me to eat healthy foods.

Ivory-billed woodpecker

The Thrill of Rediscovery

(1) The ivory-billed woodpecker is the largest woodpecker in North America. (2) For 60 years, scientists thought this woodpecker was extinct. (3) It wasn't. (4) It lived secretly in a vast area of wild Arkansas swamps. (5) One birdwatcher cried the first time he saw the bird. (6) A scientist spent months in the swamp making a video of the woodpecker. (7) Ditto taping the bird's awesome drumming. (8) An expert said that the bird shows us how lucky we are. (9) We have another chance to save this spectacular bird and its habitat. (10) Finding the bird again was a moving experience for bird lovers.

---

8 Which sentence could logically follow sentence 1?

   A. The male has a fire engine red crest on its head.

   B. It's about 20 inches tall and has a wingspan of almost a yard.

   C. It looks a lot like the smaller common woodpecker until you compare them side by side.

   D. The bird is black with white patches on its wings.

9 What is the BEST way to combine the underlined part of sentences 2 and 3?

> For 60 years, scientists thought this woodpecker was <u>extinct. It</u> wasn't.

   A. extinct it

   B. extinct, it

   C. extinct, but it

   D. extinct; in addition, it

GO ON

10 Which transition word or phrase should be added to the beginning of sentence 4?

   A. Instead,

   B. Of course,

   C. In the past,

   D. So that

11 Which sentence should logically be after sentence 4?

   A. Sentence 7

   B. Sentence 8

   C. Sentence 9

   D. Sentence 10

12 Which sentence doesn't fit the language and tone of this paragraph?

   A. Sentence 6

   B. Sentence 7

   C. Sentence 8

   D. Sentence 9

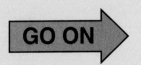

The Rodeo Today

(1) The rodeo started over 150 years ago. (2) The word *rodeo* comes from the Spanish word *rodear*. (3) First, the cowboys *rounded up*, or collected, all their cattle. (4) Cowboys led the cattle across open land to a stockyard where they were sold. (5) It was hard work. (6) In later years, cattle were shipped on railroad cars. (7) Their work was done, the cowboys had time to celebrate. (8) They held contests to see who was the best at riding, throwing ropes, and to brand cattle. (9) The first formal rodeo was held in Cheyenne, Wyoming, in 1872. (10) Cash prizes were awarded, and rules were introduced. (11) Every year, more and more people came to watch. (12) Cash prizes grew larger. (13) Along with audiences. (14) Today, rodeos are serious business, but cowboys still perform the skills they used long ago.

13 Which sentence could logically be added after sentence 2?

A. *Rodear* means to surround.

B. Cowboys learned riding skills from the Spaniards.

C. Spaniards brought horses to this country centuries ago.

D. Cowboys were also called cowpokes.

14 Which transition phrase should be added to the beginning of sentence 4?

A. From then on,

B. Before the roundup,

C. After the roundup,

D. As a result of the roundup,

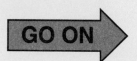

GO ON

15 Which sentence contains details that are unimportant to the paragraph?

   A. Sentence 5

   B. Sentence 6

   C. Sentence 7

   D. Sentence 8

16 What is the BEST way to rewrite sentence 7?

   A. Their work was done the cowboys had time to celebrate.

   B. Their work was done; however, the cowboys had time to celebrate.

   C. When their work was done the cowboys had time to celebrate.

   D. When their work was done, the cowboys had time to celebrate.

17 What is the BEST way to revise the underlined part of sentence 8 to create parallel structure?

> They held contests to see who was the best <u>at riding, throwing ropes, and to brand cattle.</u>

   A. at riding, to throw ropes, and to brand cattle.

   B. at riding, throwing ropes, and branding cattle.

   C. to ride, to throw ropes, and branding cattle.

   D. Make no change.

18 Which of the following is NOT a complete sentence?

   A. Sentence 10

   B. Sentence 11

   C. Sentence 12

   D. Sentence 13

19 Which sentence best states the *main idea* of the paragraph?

   A. Today's rodeo has a long history.

   B. A cattle roundup was hard work.

   C. A cowboy's skills haven't changed over the years.

   D. A rodeo is a kind of contest.

STOP. THIS IS THE END OF THE REVIEW TEST.
SEE PAGE 203 FOR ANSWERS AND EXPLANATIONS.

Chapter 6 Write Essays

Use the Writing Process

Writing a good essay takes several steps. The steps are called the Writing Process.

The Writing Process

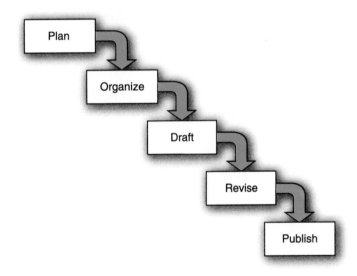

 1. **Plan** your writing. Brainstorm and write down ideas about your topic. Use a graphic organizer.

 2. **Organize** your ideas. Use an outline or organizing chart.

 3. **Draft** three to five paragraphs. Use the ideas from your outline or organizing chart.

 4. **Revise** your work. Make corrections to your draft.

 5. **Publish** your paper. Make a neat, final copy.

Step 1 Plan

Find Your Purpose

Get your ideas together before you start writing your essay. Ask yourself: *Why am I writing this? What is my purpose?* The purpose is the reason for writing the story, letter, essay, or composition.

The purpose can be to write a(n):

- **Narrative** You tell a story. It can be a story about you or someone else. It can be real or made up.

- **Persuasive Essay** You give your opinion or point of view about a controversial topic. Sometimes you ask your reader to do something, try to change your reader's mind, or give your reader advice.

- **Response to Literature** You read a poem, story, or essay and explain what it means. You use details and examples from the reading to support your ideas.

- **Expository Essay** You can explain facts about a topic or describe how something works.

Write *N* for narrative, *P* for persuasive essay, *R* for response to literature, and *E* for expository essay.

__R__ book report

____ 1. letter to the editor

____ 2. story about yourself

____ 3. how to use a camera

____ 4. essay about a poem

____ 5. the life of the president

____ 6. report about snakes

1. P; 2. N; 3. E; 4. R; 5. N; 6. E

Brainstorm Ideas

Here are several ways to brainstorm. Use the one that works best for you.

1. Write the topic at the top of the page. Then quickly **list** all your ideas about the topic. Lists are helpful with all kinds of writing.

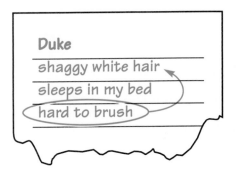

2. Use a **cluster map** to describe and group information. Cluster maps are helpful with most kinds of writing.

    Put the topic in the center circle. Draw lines to connect the ideas.

Describe your favorite animal. Explain why it is special to you.

3. Use a two-column chart to compare and contrast different sides of a topic. Two-column charts are helpful with persuasive essays and responses to literature.

The School Board wants to reduce discipline problems. They want students to wear school uniforms. What is your opinion?

School Uniforms

Pros	Cons
Everyone wears the same thing.	Kids should wear what they want.
Saves money	Uniforms are boring.
Meets dress code	Ugly and uncomfortable
My mother works at a clothing store.	Uniforms are expensive.
Uniforms help kids act better.	

Practice A: Brainstorm a list of ideas for each of the topics below. Write the lists in your notebook.

1. Describe the best moment in your life.

2. Explain the following proverb: "Beauty is only skin deep."

Practice B: In your notebook, make a cluster map for each of the topics below. Start with a circle in the middle of your paper. Write the topic in the circle. Then write your ideas. Draw arrows to connect the ideas.

1. Write about your favorite kind of food and why you like it.

2. Art is everywhere. Write about how art is important in your life.

Practice C: In your notebook, make a two-column chart for each of the topics below.

1. All students must pass a test to graduate from high school. Do you agree or disagree with this law?

2. Some people believe that television is harmful. Do you agree or disagree? Give reasons to support your opinion.

SEE PAGE 205 FOR SAMPLE RESPONSES.

Strategies for Test-Taking Success: Writing © Heinle, Cengage Learning. Photocopying this page is prohibited by law.

Step 2 Organize

Group your ideas into categories. Each category will become one paragraph in your essay. Cross out details that don't belong.

The first group is the **introduction**. Write sentences that *introduce* your main idea to the reader.

The middle group is the **body**. Write sentences that *support* your main idea. Each group or category should be about one supporting idea. For most writing tests, write two to three groups.

The last group is the **conclusion**. It is a *summary* of your ideas.

Use an **outline** or an **organizing chart** to organize your ideas.

Here is an outline for the cluster map of "My Dog Duke" on page 117. An outline shows the main idea and supporting details. Use a Roman numeral (I, II, III) for each category. Use a capital letter (A, B, C) for each supporting detail. Use a number (1, 2, 3) for each fact, example, or other piece of information under the supporting detail. Cross out details that don't belong.

Title	My Dog Duke
Introduction	I. My favorite pet is my dog Duke. A. I have other pets, but he is my favorite. B. I take care of him. C. Duke is always ready to play.

Body	II. What he looks like
	A. He is small.
	B. ~~My cousin's dog is big.~~
	C. He has shaggy white hair.
	   1. He steps on it when he walks.
	   2. Sometimes it is hard to brush.
	III. How I take care of him
	A. I give him food and fresh water.
	   1. He likes dog biscuits.
	B. We go for a walk in the park.
	C. He likes to play catch with a Frisbee.
	D. He sleeps in my bed because he's afraid of the dark.

Conclusion	IV. We have fun together. A. Duke is a funny dog. B. I love Duke.

Practice: Look at the brainstorming lists you wrote about the best moment in your life and "Beauty is only skin deep" on page 118. Pick one list and organize those ideas into an outline. Write in your notebook. Cross out any ideas that don't belong.

Use the Organizing Checklist to review your outline.

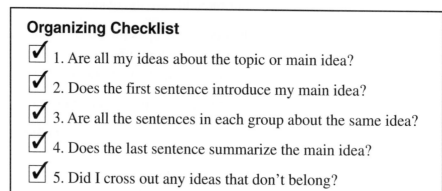

Organizing Checklist

☑ 1. Are all my ideas about the topic or main idea?

☑ 2. Does the first sentence introduce my main idea?

☑ 3. Are all the sentences in each group about the same idea?

☑ 4. Does the last sentence summarize the main idea?

☑ 5. Did I cross out any ideas that don't belong?

Here is an organizing chart for the two-column chart on "School Uniforms" on page 118. Ideas that don't fit are crossed out.

School Uniforms	
Introduction: State the issue	The principal of our school wants everyone to wear uniforms. Some people don't want school uniforms. But I think it is a good idea. It will make school easier for me.
Body Pros & reasons	I think school uniforms are a good idea because everyone wears the same thing. We don't have to worry about what to wear every day. It saves money because we just buy our uniforms and don't have to buy lots of other clothes for school. ~~My mother works in a clothing store.~~ We will always meet the dress code so we won't get in trouble.
Cons & reasons	Some people disagree. They say we have the right to choose what we wear to school. Besides, they think uniforms are ugly, uncomfortable, and expensive. School would be boring if everyone wore the same thing.
Conclusion: Explain your position	With uniforms I don't have to worry about what to wear to school. Everyone is equal. This is one reason why school uniforms will make school easier.

Practice: Look at the two-column charts you made about "All students must pass a test to graduate from high school" and "Some people believe television is harmful" on page 118. Pick one list and use it to make an organizing chart. Write in your notebook.

Use the Organizing Checklist on page 120 to review your chart.

 Step 3 Draft

Use your organizing chart to draft four or five paragraphs.

First paragraph: Start your **introduction** with a question or interesting fact. Make the reader want to know more about your topic.
Second, third, and fourth paragraphs: Each paragraph in the **body** is about one supporting idea.
Last paragraph: The **conclusion** is a summary of your ideas.

This is a draft written from the outline about "My Dog Duke" on page 119.

My Dog Duke
I have too cats and a parot, but my favirite pet is my dog, Duke is my best friend. I take care of him. We play together
Duke are a small dog he has long white hair. It is so long it touches the ground when he walks. Sometimes it trips on his own hair! He alway get things in his hair. Its hard to brush sometimes.
I take care of Duke. Everyday i give him a bowl of dog food and water. It likes dog biscuits too. Good for his teeth.
We go for a walk to the park almost every day after school. Duke likes to play catch. He likes to catch a Frisbee. He looks very funny jumping up to catch the Frisbee. Duke likes to sleep with me at night. He is scared of the dark. He hides under the blanket when he heres a lound nose.
In conclution, Duke is a funny dog. We have lots of fun together. He is my favorite pet. I love Duke very much.

Practice A: Use the outline you made for the best moment in your life or "Beauty is only skin deep" on page 120. Write a draft four to five paragraphs long in your notebook.

Practice B: Use the organizing chart you made for "All students must pass a test to graduate from high school" or "Some people believe television is harmful" on page 121. Write a draft four to five paragraphs long in your notebook.

Use the Drafting Checklist to review your draft.

Drafting Checklist

 1. Do I have four to five paragraphs?

 2. Does the first paragraph introduce my main idea?

3. Does my first sentence get my reader's attention?

4. Is each paragraph about one supporting detail?

5. Does the last paragraph summarize the main idea?

Step 4 Revise

Revise your work. Make corrections to your draft. Check for correct grammar, spelling, punctuation, and paragraph unity. Work carefully and neatly.

Look at this revision of "My Dog Duke."

---

                    two   parrot   favorite
I have ~~too~~ cats and a ~~parot~~, but my ~~favirite~~ pet is my dog. ⟨Duke is my best friend.⟩ I take

care of him. We play together. ⟵

           is   He
Duke ~~are~~ a small dog. ~~he~~ has long white hair. It is so long it touches the ground when he

              he   always gets   It's
walks. Sometimes ~~it~~ trips on his own hair! He ~~alway get~~ things in his hair. ~~Its~~ hard to brush

sometimes.

                    morning I   He
I take care of Duke. ~~Everyday i~~ give him a bowl of dog food and water. ~~It~~ likes dog
     They are good
biscuits, too. ~~Good~~ for his teeth.

                       in
We go for a walk ~~to~~ the park almost every day after school. Duke likes to play
       with   it
catch. ~~He likes to catch~~ a Frisbee. He looks very funny jumping up to catch ~~the Frisbee~~.

Duke ~~likes to~~ sleeps with me at night. He is scared of the dark. He hides under the blanket
           hears loud noise
when he ~~heres~~ a ~~lound nose~~.
     conclusion
In ~~conelution~~, Duke is a funny dog. We have lots of fun together. He is my favorite pet. I

love Duke very much.

Practice A: Edit this paragraph.

Im not Shy

Kids on school think I am very shy. I'm quit and dont talk much. They don't know me too good. I talk to the teacher. I say answers when I no I'm right. I not shy an home. I talk a lot with my brother. We laughs and plays together. I tell him everything. My brother knows me very well. He knows I'm not shy.

Use the Revision Checklist after you revise your draft.

Revision Checklist

☑ 1. Is there an introduction, a body, and a conclusion?

☑ 2. Do my subjects and verbs agree?

☑ 3. Are the spelling and punctuation correct?

☑ 4. Can I use better words?

☑ 5. Are my paragraphs in a logical order?

☑ 6. Did I use transitions to connect my ideas?

☑ 7. Can I add information?

☑ 8. Do all the sentences belong?

SEE PAGE 206 FOR REVISIONS.

Practice B: Revise your draft about the best moment in your life or "Beauty is only skin deep" on page 122.

Use the Revision Checklist on page 124 to revise your draft.

Practice C: Revise your draft about "All students must pass a test to graduate from high school" or "Some people believe television is harmful" on page 122.

Use the Revision Checklist on page 124 to revise your draft.

 Step 5 Publish

Publishing means you will write a **final copy** with all your revisions and corrections. Write neatly and clearly. This is the essay your audience or grader will see. Use a computer if you can.

> My Dog Duke
> by Chang Wook Heo
>
> I have two cats and a parrot, but my favorite pet is my dog. I take care of him. We play together. Duke is my best friend.
>
> Duke is a small dog. He has long white hair. It is so long it...

Practice D: In your notebook, write a final copy of your essay about the best moment in your life or "Beauty is only skin deep" above. Make all your revisions.

Use the Publishing Checklist below to review your final copy.

Publishing Checklist

☑ 1. Did I include all my revisions and corrections?

☑ 2. Do I have a title?

☑ 3. Did I indent the paragraphs?

☑ 4. Is my handwriting neat and easy to read?

TIP

Don't be afraid to make changes. This is your chance to improve your work.

Write a Biographical Narrative

Biographical Narrative

A **biographical narrative** is a story about a person. If you write about yourself, it's called an *autobiographical narrative.*

Here are some questions, or writing prompts, for autobiographical narratives:

- What was your first day at school like?

- What are your memories of your earliest years?

- Friends are very important. Who is your best friend and why?

- Who is your role model? What qualities does he or she have that make this person a role model for you?

Use the five steps of the Writing Process to write an autobiographical narrative.

> **Writing Task:** What is special about your family's culture? Write a narrative explaining important features of your background.

PLAN

Get your ideas for the topic by brainstorming. Use one of the methods described on pages 116–117.

ORGANIZE

Group your ideas into categories. Use an outline or organizing chart. Cross out details that don't belong. Use the Organizing Checklist on page 120 to review your work.

TIP

Don't forget to title your work and write your name on it.

	I am from Greece
Introduction	My family is Greece. We have different customs and speak a different language. We have different holidays and eat different foods. People think I'm strange. I'm really lucky.
Body	My grandparents dont speak English. We speak greek. I go to Greek school. Knowing greek helped me learn english words. ~~My neighbors are from Korea.~~ We have different holidays. Easter comes on a different day than in America. We have red easter eggs and play a game with them. My mother cooks really good greek food. I love it. It is healthy. We have desserts with honey and eat lots of olives and cheese. It is delicious.
Conclusion	I am both Greek and American, so I have the best of both. I am lucky.

DRAFT

Using your outline or organizing chart, write your ideas in paragraphs. Use the Drafting Checklist on page 122 to review your draft.

I come from Greece

My family is Greece. We practis Greek customs. We speek a different Language. We celebrate different holidays and eat different kinds of foods. Some people think I am strange. I think I am lucky.

My grandparents dont speak English very well. We speek Greek at home. My grandmother taught me the Greek alphabet. In third grade I go to Greek lessons after school. Many english words come from Greek words. It is easy for me to learn new english words because I know Greek.

Greek traditions is very old. Some holidays are different we celebrate Easter on a different day. We don't have Easter egg hunts. On Eastermorning there are red eggs. We play a game and try to crack everyone's egg.

REVISE

Revise your work. Make corrections on your draft. Write neatly. Check for correct grammar, spelling, punctuation, and paragraph unity. Use the Revision Checklist on page 124 to revise your draft.

C
I come from Greece

Greek   practice   speak
My family is ~~Greece~~. We ~~practis~~ Greek customs. We ~~speek~~ a

I
different ~~Language~~. We celebrate different holidays and eat different

kinds of foods. Some people think I am strange. I think I am lucky.

speak
My grandparents don't speak English very well. We ~~speek~~ Greek

at home. My grandmother taught me the Greek alphabet. In third

went   English
grade, I ~~go~~ to Greek lessons after school. Many ~~eglish~~ words

English
come from Greek words. It is easy for me to learn new ~~english~~ words

because I know Greek.

are   We
Greek traditions ~~is~~ very old. Some holidays are different. ~~we~~

celebrate Easter on a different day. We don't have Easter egg hunts.

morning
On Easter, there are red eggs. We play a game and try to crack

eggs
everyone's ~~egg~~.

cooks   spinach
My mother ~~cook~~ Greek food. I love Greek ~~spinich~~ and cheese pie.

in
Desserts have honey ~~at~~ them. We eat lots of olives and cheese. ~~I like~~

~~hamburgers and French fries, too~~. I love vegetables and other healthy

foods. Greek food is delicious.

I'm
In conclusion, because I am Greek, ~~Im~~ different from

many kids at school. (That's special.) I am American and Greek.

PUBLISH

On a writing test, you would now rewrite your essay with all your revisions and corrections. Write neatly and clearly. This is the essay your audience or grader will see. Use a computer if you can. Use the Publishing Checklist on page 125 to review your corrections.

Biographical and autobiographical narratives are often in chronological order. This means that you write about the events in the order in which they happened.

Use time-order transitions like *first, next, then, after that, afterwards,* and *finally* to help put your ideas in chronological order.

Answer the questions.

Example: When do you get up in the morning? 6:30

    A. When do you eat lunch? _____

    B. When do you go to school? _____

    C. When do you take a shower or bath? _____

    D. When do you eat dinner? _____

    E. When do you go to bed? _____

    F. When do you have English class? _____

    G. When do you exercise? _____

    H. When do you do homework? _____

Now put your answers in chronological order. Write in your notebook.

Practice: Use your chronological list to write an autobiographical essay. Use the Writing Process. Write in your notebook.

Writing Task: Write about a typical day in your life.

 PLAN

Brainstorm your topic.

ORGANIZE

Use time-order transitions to organize your ideas. Copy and complete the chart below into your notebook. Use the Organizing Checklist on page 120 to review your organizing chart.

A Typical Day in My Life	
Introduction	
Body	
Conclusion	

 DRAFT

Write your draft in your notebook. Write four to five paragraphs. Use the Drafting Checklist on page 122 to review your draft.

 REVISE

Revise your work. Make corrections on your draft. Check for correct grammar, spelling, punctuation, and paragraph unity. Work carefully and neatly. Use the Revision Checklist on page 124 to review your corrections.

 PUBLISH

Make a final copy. Rewrite your essay with all the revisions and corrections. Write neatly and clearly. This is the paper your audience or grader will see. Use a computer if you can. Use the Publishing Checklist on page 125 to review your corrections.

Persuasive Essay

A **persuasive essay**

- asks the reader to do something
- tries to change the reader's mind
- gives the reader advice

Persuasive writing sometimes includes different sides of a topic (the pros and cons).

One form of persuasive writing is the **business letter**. It uses a more formal tone than a friendly letter. It looks different, too.

Use the business-letter format to write to:

- a company to compliment or complain about a product
- your elected officials to express your opinion about a new law
- the editor of your school or city newspaper to state your opinion about an issue or subject

> **TIP**
>
> When you write a business letter be clear and concise. Write the most important details, examples, or reasons first.

Your information ⟶ 1234 Lakeside Drive
Newark, NJ 07104
Date ⟶ March 23, 2006

Company's name and address
↓

Smith Sisters Construction Company
1700 Main Street
Newark, NJ 07104

Dear Ms. Smith, ⟵ Salutation

   I am writing to express my concern over the new building that your company is planning. It is near my house, and I think it will ruin the neighborhood.

   One major problem is traffic. This is already a busy street, and your building will cause even more traffic. It will be dangerous for children to cross the street to go to the nearby school.

   The construction will also cause problems. Loud noise, dust, and dirt are not welcomed. What can you do to ease these problems?

   My neighbors and I are going to the City Council meeting next month. We look forward to hearing your answer to these questions.

Sincerely,
Sara Wong ⟵ Your name

Read the newspaper article below. Then check the correct answer.

Bonny Burger Coming to Hillside

The Hillside City Council approved a plan to build a new Bonny Burger Drive-Through restaurant. It passed with a 5-2 majority. Both councillors who voted against it live in the neighborhood.

Beulah Guerrero said, "They'll tear down homes and local businesses. Traffic will increase. And think of all the noise and pollution it will cause." Many local residents agree.

Bonny Burger president, Emilio Rodriquez, was happy that the plan was approved. "Bonny Burger makes the biggest hamburgers for the lowest price. The restaurant will bring many new jobs to the neighborhood. So will the construction. And we will pay to make the roads better. Bonny Burger will be good for Hillside."

Phase One will begin in about two months. First, the company will tear down a small supermarket

and four houses. The demolition will make room for the restaurant and a large parking lot.

Bayview Avenue will be closed for one month. The city will dig holes in the street for new water, sewer, and power lines. Traffic will go down Pine Street instead.

You live in Hillside, and you write to express your opinion about Bonny Burger coming to town. To whom do you write?

    A. the city council

    B. the governor

    C. a neighbor

ANSWER: A

Write a business letter. Use the Writing Process.

Imagine that you live in Hillside, and you read the newspaper article on page 132. What is your opinion of building a new Bonny Burger restaurant in your neighborhood? Write a letter to the Hillside City Council and express your opinion.

 PLAN

Get your ideas for the topic by brainstorming. Use one of the methods discussed on pages 116–117.

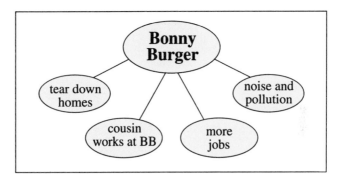

 ORGANIZE

Group your ideas into pros and cons. Use an outline or organizing chart. Cross out details that don't belong. Use the Organizing Checklist on page 120 to review your work.

DRAFT

Use your outline or organizing chart to draft four to five paragraphs. Use the Drafting Checklist on page 122 to review your draft.

Introduction	I am disappoint to read about the new Bonny Burger restaurant coming to Hillside.
Body	The restaurant will bring traffice. This means more noise and pollutin. Our neighborhood will

TIP

Use polite language in a business letter.

136 Bayview Ave.
Hillside, TX 78240
October 30, 2007

Hillside City Council
City Hall
456 Main Street
Hillside, TX 78240

Dear City Council Members,

I am disappoint to read in the newpaper that Bonny Burger will build a resturant on my street. Beulah Guerrero was right to vote against it. It was not be good for the neighborhood.

The resturant will bring more traffic more noise and pollution. Bayview avenue will never be the same. It will be dangerous for children to cross the street. It will no longer be quiet and peaceful.

It is good that they will add more power and water lines to the area. But this neighborhod has lots of old houses. Some will tear down. This is not good. The new modern building will not fit n and will look ugly.

We dont need anew resturant here. We need the supermarket and job. Please to think of a better way to improve our neighborhood than bring in a fast-food resturant tht sells terrible handburgers.

Sincerely,

Julio Rossi

REVISE

Practice A: Revise Julio Rossi's letter. Make corrections on the draft. Check for correct grammar, spelling, punctuation, and paragraph unity. Work carefully and neatly. Use the Business Letter Checklist below to review your revisions.

Business Letter Checklist

☑ 1. Is my letter in the correct form?
☑ 2. Does the introduction describe the issue?
☑ 3. Does the body support my opinion?
☑ 4. Does the conclusion summarize the issue and ask for a definite solution?
☑ 5. Is my writing polite?
☑ 6. Is the address correct?

PUBLISH

Practice B: Make a final copy of Julio Rossi's letter in your notebook. Make all your revisions and corrections. Write neatly and clearly. This is important practice for the writing test. Use a computer if you can. Use the Publishing Checklist on page 125 to review your corrections.

SEE PAGE 207 FOR REVISIONS.

Practice C: In your notebook, write a persuasive business letter. Use the Writing Process.

Writing Task: Your state senator wants to raise the minimum wage. Write a letter to the editor of your town newspaper expressing your opinion about this issue.

PLAN

Get your ideas for the topic by brainstorming. Use one of the methods on pages 116–117.

ORGANIZE

Group your ideas into categories. Use an outline or organizing chart. Each category will become one paragraph when you write your draft. Cross out details that don't belong. Use the Organizing Checklist on page 120 to review your work.

DRAFT

Use your outline or organizing chart to draft the business letter in your notebook. Use examples and facts to support your opinion. Use the Drafting Checklist on page 122 to review your draft.

REVISE

Revise your letter. Make corrections on the draft. Check for correct grammar, spelling, punctuation, and paragraph unity. Work carefully and neatly. Use the Business Letter Checklist on page 135 to review your letter.

PUBLISH

Make a final copy. In your notebook, rewrite the letter with all your revisions and corrections. Write neatly and clearly. This is the letter your audience or grader will see. Use a computer if you can. Use the Publishing Checklist on page 125 to review your corrections.

Response to Literature

A response to literature is an essay or composition about a work of literature. It answers a question about:

- the characters

- the plot

- a specific section of the reading

Use the Writing Process when you write your response to literature. Your essay or composition will have three parts:

1. **Introduction:** Introduce the topic. Be sure to give the title of the work of literature and the author's name. The introduction is usually one paragraph.

2. **Body:** Give specific information and examples from the reading to support your ideas. The body is usually one, two, or three paragraphs.

3. **Conclusion:** Summarize the topic. The conclusion is usually one paragraph.

Read the story "The Hairy Arm" on page 138.

The Hairy Arm
An Ancient Japanese Tale

1   A man named Sukeyasu was on his way home from the capital city. He stopped for the night at an ancient temple. A villager warned him that the temple was haunted. The villager said that people who stayed there disappeared. However, Sukeyasu ignored the man and went to bed. The snow was blowing outside, and the temple had no heat. Sukeyasu thought about ghosts. He shivered in the dark.

2   Late in the night, Sukeyasu heard the sound of strange voices outside. Peering through a hole in the wall, he saw that the garden was white with snow. He also saw the dark shape of a man as tall as the roof. Suddenly, a skinny, hairy arm came through the hole like a snake and touched his face. Sukeyasu jumped back, and the arm disappeared.

3   Sukeyasu curled up in a ball. He waited and watched the hole. The next time the hairy arm came through the hole, Sukeyasu grabbed it. He was stronger than the creature and tied its arm to a chair. Then he lit a torch and went outside to find the owner of the arm. He thought to himself, "The creature looked as tall as the roof, but it must be small indeed. It's arm fit through the hole in the wall."

4   Finally, the creature let out a squeak. It was an old badger! In the morning, Sukeyasu showed it to the villagers.

5   Nothing haunted the temple after that.

Write a response to "The Hairy Arm." Use the Writing Process.

> **Writing Task:** Describe the main character. What kind of man is Sukeyasu? Give examples from the story to support your description.

 PLAN

Get your ideas for the topic by brainstorming. Use one of the methods discussed on pages 116–117.

Sukeyasu
strong
faces his fears
doesn't listen to villagers
hungry

 ORGANIZE

Group your ideas into categories. Use an outline or organizing chart. Cross out details that don't belong. Use the Organizing Checklist on page 120 to review your work.

Title

Introduction

Body

Conclusion

Description of the Main Character in "The Hairy Arm"
I. Sukeyasu is the main character.
   A. independent
   B. brave
   C. helps the villagers
II. How he is independent
   A. He doesn't pay attention to the villager's story.
   B. He stays in the temple even though he is cold and afraid.
   C. Maybe he was hungry.
III. How he is brave
   A. tries to find out who makes strange noises
   B. Even though he is worried, he looks out the hole.
   C. The arm touches him, but he doesn't yell or run away.
   D. grabs the creature's arm and ties it to a chair
   E. He wants to find out what the creature is.
IV. Sukeyasu's character helped the villagers.
   A. They were afraid.
   B. Because Sukeyasu was independent and brave, the villagers learned what the creature really was.

Practice A: DRAFT Use the outline on page 139 to draft a response to "The Hairy Arm." Write in your notebook. Use the Response to Literature below to review your draft.

Response to Literature Checklist:
- ☑ 1. Did I read the passage carefully?
- ☑ 2. Did I read the writing prompt carefully?
- ☑ 3. Did I organize my essay with an introduction, a body, and a conclusion?
- ☑ 4. Did I use examples and details from the work of literature to support my main idea?
- ☑ 5. Is my essay interesting?

Practice B: REVISE

Revise your writing. Make corrections on your draft. Check for correct grammar, spelling, punctuation, and paragraph unity. Work carefully and neatly. Use the Revision Checklist on page 124 to review your edits.

SEE PAGE 207 FOR SAMPLE DRAFT AND REVISION.

PUBLISH

Make a final copy. Rewrite your essay with all your revisions and corrections. Write neatly and clearly. This is the essay your audience or grader will see. Use a computer if you can. Use the Publishing Checklist on page 125 to review your corrections.

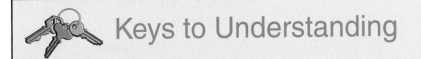

Keys to Understanding

Response to Literature

Read the piece of literature carefully. You may need to read it more than once.

Underline or circle the following things so you can find them again quickly:

- Words or phrases that make a picture in your mind

- A character's feelings

- Feelings the writer wants *you* to feel

- Special information about the characters or setting

Read the poem. Then complete the writing task on page 142.

A Book[1]

He ate and drank the precious[2] words,
His spirit grew robust.[3]
He soon forgot that he was poor,
And that his bones were dust.

He danced along the gloomy days,
And his present of wings
Was but a book. What liberty
An unchained spirit brings!

---

[1] Adapted from Emily Dickinson, "A Book."
[2] **precious**: extremely valuable; much loved
[3] **robust**: strong, healthy, vigorous

Practice: Write a response to "A Book" in your notebook. Use the Writing Process.

> **Writing Task:** Describe how the boy in this poem changes when he reads a book. What do you think he was like before he read a book? How can you tell? What happens to him after he reads the book? Give examples from the poem to support your ideas.

 PLAN

Get ideas for your essay by brainstorming. Use one of the methods discussed on pages 116–117.

 ORGANIZE

Group your ideas into categories. Use an outline or organizing chart. Cross out details that don't belong. Use the Organizing Checklist on page 120 to review your work.

 DRAFT

Use your outline or organizing chart to draft four to five paragraphs. Use the Drafting Checklist on page 122 to review your draft.

 REVISE

Revise your response. Make corrections on your draft. Check for correct grammar, spelling, punctuation, and paragraph unity. Work carefully and neatly. Use the Revision Checklist on page 124 to review your corrections.

 PUBLISH

On a writing test you would now write your final essay, making the corrections from your edits. Check your final essay with the Publishing Checklist on page 125.

SEE PAGE 208 FOR SAMPLE OUTLINE AND REVISION.

Strategy 26

Write an Expository Essay

Expository Essay

An **expository essay** explains facts about a topic, how something works, or why something happened.

The information in expository essays is often in chronological order.

Sample topics for expository essays may include:

- Describe an event and explain what caused it.

- Describe an event and explain its effect.

- Explain how something works.

- Explain how to make or do something.

- Explain facts about something in nature.

An expository essay is factual.

Write an expository essay. Use the Writing Process.

> **Writing Task:** Describe the history of the state you live in or a state you know.

PLAN

Get ideas for your essay by brainstorming. Use one of the methods discussed on pages 116–117.

Kentucky History

15th state (1792)

part of Virginia

famous people from Kentucky

Lincoln was born in 1809.

Mary Todd Lincoln lived in Lexington.

ORGANIZE

Group your ideas into categories. Use an outline or organizing chart. Cross out details that don't belong. Use the Organizing Checklist on page 120 to review your work.

The History of Kentucky	
Introduction	One of the oldest territories in the US. Long history with important people. Many traditions still today.
Body	Kentucky first part of virginia. In 1792 it was the 15th state First settlers around the 1770s.
	Many famous people lived in Kentucky. Abraham Lincoln born there. His wife, Mary Todd, lived in Lexington until she married Abraham Lincoln. ~~Two sisters in Lexington wrote, "Happy Birthday to You."~~ Stephen Foster wrote "My Old Kentucky Home" while visiting his cousin who lived there.
	Now Kentucky is most famous for horse racing, Kentucky Derby. It is called the bluegrass state, because the limestone in the ground makes the grass look blue. Good for horses, who eat bluegrass.
Conclusion	Kentucky is an interesting state with a long rich history. Come visit sometime.

TIP

Expository essays are factual. Present your information in logical order.

DRAFT

Use your outline or organizing chart to draft four to five paragraphs. Use the Drafting Checklist on page 122 to review your draft.

The History of Kentucky

Have you ever been to Kentucky. Kentucky is one of the oldes territories in the United states. It has a long history and many famous people lived there. Its rich with traditions, such as horse racing.

Kentucky is first part of virginia. In 1792 it become the 15th state to join the union. Settlers went there starting around 1770s. Later Kentucky played an important role in the Civil War and the underground railroad.

Lots of famous people lived in Kentucky. Abraham Lincoln was born there. Hs wife, Mary Todd, lived in Lexington until she married. Stephen Foster wrote "My Old Kentucky Home" while visiting his cousin.

Now Kentucky is most famous for a horse race called the Kentucky Derby. Kentucky is the Blusegrass state because of the limestone in the ground. It makes the grass look blue. It is good for the horse who get strong from eating the bluegrass.

Kentucky is a very interesting state. It has a long, rich history. It was the home of many historic Americans. And the bluegrass is beutiful. Please come visit.

Practice: REVISE Revise the draft of "The History of Kentucky." Check for correct grammar, spelling, punctuation, and paragraph unity. Work carefully and neatly. Use the Revision Checklist on page 124 to review your corrections.

SEE PAGE 208 FOR A SAMPLE REVISION.

PUBLISH

On the writing test, you would now make your final copy using the Publishing Checklist on page 125 to review your corrections.

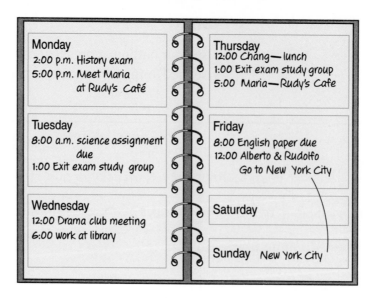

Monday
2:00 p.m. History exam
5:00 p.m. Meet Maria
          at Rudy's Café

Tuesday
8:00 a.m. science assignment
          due
1:00 Exit exam study group

Wednesday
12:00 Drama club meeting
6:00 work at library

Thursday
12:00 Chang—lunch
1:00 Exit exam study group
5:00 Maria—Rudy's Cafe

Friday
8:00 English paper due
12:00 Alberto & Rudolfo
          Go to New York City

Saturday

Sunday   New York City

Writing Task: This is Silesh's date book. He has a busy schedule. Read it carefully. Write an expository essay describing Silesh's week. Write in your notebook.

PLAN

Use information from Silesh's date book in your essay.

ORGANIZE

Use the Organizing Checklist on page 120 to review your organizing chart.

DRAFT

Use the Drafting Checklist on page 122 to review your draft.

REVISE

Use the Revision Checklist on page 124 to review your corrections.

PUBLISH

Use the Publishing Checklist on page 125 to review your corrections.

CHAPTER 6: REVIEW TEST

Mark your answers on the Answer Grid.

1   **Revise the following text. Then make a final copy in your notebook.**

How to Whistle

Do you know how to whistle. If you dont, here are three easy steps to follow. Practice them. I promise you will be whistling in no time.

First, make a tiny circle with your lips. Just big enough for air can pass threw. Next, put the tip of your tongue behind your bottom teeth. Third, blow out air through your mouth. Try not to blow to hard. Its easier to whistle with a small amount of air. To make your first note. You may have to move your tongue or the circle formed by your lips.

Since you can make a sound it's time to experiment. Change the strength of your breath to produce other note. Above all, practice. You will be whistle your favorite songs.

---

2   **Name the five steps of the Writing Process. Then write one or two sentences that describe what you do in each step. Write in your notebook.**

Step 1.

Step 2.

Step 3.

Step 4.

Step 5.

GO ON

Board Bans Sugary Soft Drinks

1   The Cane County School Board banned soft drinks from school vending machines. The board was under pressure from many groups that fight childhood obesity. The decision is going to create controversy.

2   "Kids are drinking and eating too much sugar these days. It's just not healthy," said dr. Fernando Cruz. "We need to limit students' choices to healthy ones. Juice and milk will help build strong, healthy young people."

3   School vending machines will have only bottled water, milk, and they can have fruit juices. "We can't teach about healthy habits in the classroom and offer them sugary drinks outside in the hallways," said Supervisor Kim Leung.

4   Ben Sweetman criticized the ban. His is from the group Freedom for Kids' Choice. This group beleives students need to learn to make their own choices. "If we try to control their choices, they'll just overdo it when they have the chance. The obesity problem will get worse, not better," he said. "After all, this is a free country."

5   Marta Gonzales voted against the ban. She was the only board member to vote against it. She is looking into the economic impact on the school district. "The sodas were an important source of income for the schools. Now we may have to raise taxes to make up for it," she said.

---

3   **What change, if any, should be made to this sentence?**

> "It's just not healthy," said dr. Fernando Cruz.

A   Delete the apostrophe in *It's*

B   Insert *the* after *said*

C   Change *dr.* to *Dr.*

D   Leave as is.

4   **Which transition word or phrase should be added to the beginning of paragraph 3?**

A   Until now,

B   Before the vote,

C   Under the new rules,

D   As each board member voted,

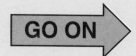

5 How should the underlined part of this sentence be rewritten to create a parallel structure?

> School vending machines will have only <u>bottled water, milk, and they can have fruit juices.</u>

A bottled water, milk, and fruit juices.

B bottled water, they can have milk and fruit juices.

C bottled water milk and they can have fruit juices.

D Leave as is.

6 What is the correct way to spell the underlined word?

> This group <u>beleives</u> students need to learn to make our own choices.

A beleeves

B believes

C beleaves

D Leave as is.

7 What is the BEST way to combine these sentences?

> Marta Gonzales voted against the ban. She was the only board member to vote against it.

A Marta Gonzales voted against the ban, she was the only board member to vote against it.

B Marta Gonzales was the only board member to vote against the ban.

C Marta Gonzales, who was the only board member to vote, was against the ban.

D Marta Gonzales voted against the ban; however; she was the only board member to vote against it.

8 Reread the article "Board Bans Sugary Soft Drinks."

> **Writing Task:** In your notebook, write a letter to the Cane County School Board expressing your opinion. Use the Writing Process. Show your work at each stage of the process.

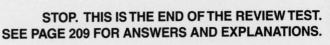

STOP. THIS IS THE END OF THE REVIEW TEST.
SEE PAGE 209 FOR ANSWERS AND EXPLANATIONS.

Chapter 7

Put It All Together

Strategy 27 Write a Good Short Answer

Short Answers

A good short answer answers a specific question or gives an opinion. It often gives supporting details, examples, or reasons. A short answer can be as short as two sentences or as long as a paragraph.

To answer a short-answer question:
1. Read carefully to understand what information it asks for.
2. Underline key words to help you focus.
3. Start your answer by including key words from the question.
4. Give a specific example, reason, or explanation.

You may be asked to write about specific information in a reading. These answers will be only one or two sentences.

> **TIP**
>
> Short answers take between 5 and 15 minutes to read, plan, and answer.

Question	Short Answer
How many applications does NASA get for its astronaut program each year?	NASA gets over 2,000 applications for its astronaut program each year.

Sometimes you will be asked to write about a narrative, a letter, a work of literature, or an essay. These answers can be up to a paragraph long. Use a shortened form of the Writing Process (explained below) to organize your ideas into a paragraph.

 PLAN Brainstorm and list ideas about your topic.

Topic: Who is your best friend? Why is he or she your best friend?

> Lueng
> helps me study - biology exam
> looks after me
> best friends look after each other

Strategy 27   Write a Good Short Answer   **151**

Number and label the items on your list:

1. topic sentence

2. supporting ideas-example

3. conclusion

Lueng	
helps me study - biology exam	2a. example
looks after me	1. topic sentence
best friends look after each other	3. conclusion
older guys bullying me	2b. example
sick - e-mailed my homework to me	2c. example

Begin your draft with a clear answer to the question. This answer is your main idea or topic sentence.

Question	Topic Sentence
Who is your best friend?	Lueng is my best friend.

Then add a strong reason or interesting example.

Question:	**Why is he or she your best friend?**
Weak reason:	Lueng is my best friend because he is nice.
Stronger reason:	Lueng is my best friend because he looks out for me.

Read the topic sentences below. Rewrite the topic sentences to make them stronger.

Topic 1: Some people think watching TV is a waste of time. Do you agree or disagree?

Weak reason: I like watching TV.
Stronger reason: _____

Topic 2: Compare and contrast a CD-ROM and a DVD.

Weak reason: A CD-ROM and a DVD look alike.
Stronger reason: _____

Sample Answers: 1. Watching TV can be educational. 2. Although they look alike, CD-ROMs and DVDs do different things.

Strategies for Test-Taking Success: Writing © Heinle, Cengage Learning. Photocopying this page is prohibited by law.

Add specific examples to support your topic sentence.[1]

Lueng is my best friend because he looks out for me.

Example 1: He is helping me study for my biology test.

Example 2: When I got the flu, he e-mailed my homework.

Example 3: Older guys bully me; Leung stands by me.

Write *S* for a specific example. Write *W* for a weak example.

_____ 1. Many universities now offer courses through TV.

_____ 2. Watching TV is fun.

_____ 3. We use CD-ROMs and DVDs at school.

_____ 4. CD-ROMs and DVDs both contain digital data.

1. S; 2. W; 3. W; 4. S

Copy the topic sentences you wrote on page 152 in your notebook. Then add two or three examples.

Example: I learn about current events when I watch the news.

End your paragraph with a summary statement that states your main idea in a new way. This is the conclusion of your paragraph.

Topic: Who is your best friend? Why is he or she your best friend?

Conclusion: Best friends look out for each other, and Lueng is the best.

Write conclusions for the paragraphs you started above.

1. **Topic:** Some people think watching TV is a waste of time. Do you agree or disagree?

   Conclusion: _____

2. **Topic:** Compare and contrast a CD-ROM and a DVD.

   Conclusion: _____

[1] To review topic sentences, see pages 91–92 in chapter 5, Strategy 17.

REVISE

Read your answer again. Make corrections. Be sure you write neatly.

Don't forget to use transitions to connect your sentences.[2] Transitions help the audience understand the move from:

the topic sentence ⟶ to a supporting detail

from one idea in a paragraph ⟶ to the next idea

from the last idea ⟶ to the conclusion

Use the **Revision Checklist for Short Answers** to check your paragraph.

My Best Friend
by Jozafa Jacob

Lueng is my best friend **because** he looks out for me.

    is

He ∧ always there when I need him. **For example**, he helped me

study for my biology test. **Then**, when I got the flu, he e-mailed

        didn't

my homework, so I ~~don't~~ fall behind in class. **But the best**

                    to

example is the time a bunch of older boys tried ~~too~~ bully me.

   stood *and eventually,* *left* *alone*

Leung ~~stand~~ by me, ∧ they ~~leave~~ me ~~by myself~~. **In conclusion**,

        look

best friends looks out for each other, ∧ and Lueng is the best.

Revision Checklist for Short Answers

☑ 1. Did I answer the question?

☑ 2. Are my examples clear?

☑ 3. Did I use correct grammar, spelling, and punctuation?

☑ 4. Did I use precise words?

☑ 5. Did I use transitions to connect ideas?

---

[2] To review transitions, see pages 100–102 in Chapter 5, Strategy 19.

Strategies for Test-Taking Success: Writing © Heinle, Cengage Learning. Photocopying this page is prohibited by law.

Practice A: Revise your short-answer paragraphs for the topics below. Use transitions to connect your sentences. Use the Revision Checklist for Short Answers on page 154 to check your work.

Topic 1: Some people think watching TV is a waste of time. Do you agree or disagree?

Topic 2: Compare and contrast a CD-ROM and a DVD.

Practice B: Examine the picture below. In your notebook, write a **narrative** paragraph about it. Tell who the people are. Describe what they are doing and how they are doing it.

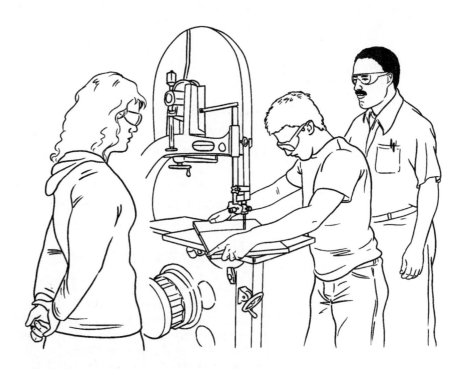

Practice C: Read the topic below. In your notebook, write a **persuasive** paragraph.

Topic: Your sports team wants to sell cell phones to students to raise money. Do you think this is a good idea? Explain why or why not.

Practice D: Read the story below. In your notebook, write a paragraph that **responds to the story**. Use details and examples from the story to support your ideas.

> **Writing Task:** Explain the purpose of exaggeration in storytelling.

Everyone knows that a fisherman exaggerates. He always says, "It was so-o-o big." He holds his hands wide to show the enormous size of the one that got away. Some people say that he is lying. The fish was not really as big as the fisherman says. He exaggerates the size. This is a point that all storytellers understand. Exaggeration tells the audience what is important. When the fisherman felt the pull of the fish on the line, he got very excited. When he tells his story, he wants to share his excitement. The size of the fish is not as important as the excitement.

Practice E: Read the article below. In your notebook, write an *expository* paragraph to answer the question below. Use information and examples from the article to support your ideas.

> **Question:** What are the benefits of using siginate in foods?

Slim Down on Seaweed

Junk food can be made healthy, thanks to a chemical from seaweed. According to scientists, the fiber in cakes, pies, and hamburgers can be increased by adding siginate, which comes from seaweed.

High-fiber diets have been shown to reduce heart disease and stomach cancer. Because siginate has no taste or smell, it does not interfere with a food's flavor. People won't notice that it is in their favorite foods.

Siginate may also cut down on obesity. It forms a lump in people's stomachs and makes them feel full. As a result, they won't want to eat too much.

"It is hard to change people's eating habits," says one scientist. "It is easier to improve the foods they normally eat."

SEE PAGE 211 FOR SAMPLE ANSWERS.

Write Longer Essays

Some tests will ask you to write an essay four to five paragraphs long. Essays are also called open responses, extended responses, or writing tasks. These tests may ask you to write narratives, persuasive essays, responses to literature, or expository essays.

Remember to use the five steps of the Writing Process[3] to write longer essays. The Writing Process will help you write a better essay. You may need to show your work from the different steps in the Writing Process on a state writing test.

Look at the web page below and the three essays that follow it. The essays are by three different students. There are examples of a very good essay, a fair essay, and a poor essay.

As you read the essays on pages 159–161, look at the Grader's Notes. These notes show you the kinds of things graders are looking for when they read your essay.

Read the web page. Then complete the Writing Task.

HOME	**Joshua Tree National Park in Distress**
NEWS	The Joshua Tree National Park has a problem. No one imagined this problem when the park opened in 1936. People used to visit the huge park in the Mojave Desert for its beautiful scenery and pure air. The air was so clean that people with lung problems went there to get well. But that's no longer true. Today, the wind carries air pollution to the park. It comes from Los Angeles and San Bernardino which are many miles away. As a result, Joshua Tree has some of the dirtiest air of any national park in the country. The polluted air is damaging the water, soil, plants, and animals, including humans.

[3] To review the Writing Process, see pages 115–125 in Chapter 6, Strategy 22.

High Ozone Levels

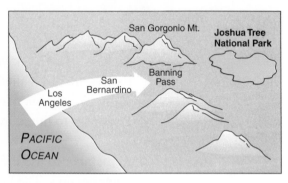

A major problem at Joshua Tree is the increased ozone in the air. Ozone is an invisible gas. It is found miles above the Earth's surface. There, it protects us from the sun's harmful rays. However, when ozone is too close to the Earth, it can damage our lungs. People who have breathing problems must limit their outdoor activities if there is a lot of ozone in the air. It can hurt children and old people, too.

Millions of cars and trucks are the main cause of high ozone levels. These vehicles produce waste products, called emissions. These emissions contain ozone. Power plants, factories, and seaports add to the ozone problem. In time, this dirty air drifts over Joshua Tree National Park, and the park's air gets polluted.

The National Park Service wants the public to know about the problem. Then people can work to improve it. Joshua Tree National Park can return to its pure state. We should not take its breathtaking beauty for granted.

Writing Task: Think about the problem of air pollution in Joshua Tree National Park. Then decide on a solution to the problem. Use information on the web page and from science you have learned in school.

Write an essay that explains the problem and gives your solution. Use information and vocabulary from the text to support your main idea. Give details and examples.

Sample 1

Joshua Tree Needs Help

Do you believe the desert has clean air? In fact, the air in Joshua Tree National Park in the Mojave Desert is polluted. Dirty air comes from gas cars and trucks in the cities. One good solution to this problem is hibrid cars and trucks.

A long time ago, sick people went to Joshua Tree for its pure air. But today the ozone in the air can hurt them. High ozone starts in cities because of gas vehicles that send emissions into the air. Then the wind is blowing dirty air into Joshua Tree. Dirty air in the park hurts plants, animals, and makes people sick.

Unless we are going to stop driving, we need to drive hibred cars. There are very few hibreds around because people don't know how good they are. For instance, they go as fast as regular cars. They don't need to be plugged in. Most important, hibrid vehicles don't put emissions into the air. Even if we drive a lot hibrids cars keep the air cleaner. As a result the air over Joshua Tree will be cleaner, too.

In conclusion, we need to reduce pollution for our health and clean air in Joshua Tree. Hibrids will be good for the park and good for people.

Grader's Notes

✔+ good title

✔+ interesting question

✔+ clear main idea

✔ addresses both problem and solution

✗ minor spelling error

✔+ body with 2 paragraphs

✔++ uses ideas from text and from own knowledge

✔+ uses new vocabulary

✗ verb tense

✗ parallel structure problem

✔ good transition

✔+ gives examples and details

✗ commas in complex sentences introductory phrases

✔ concluding paragraph

✔ topic sentence

✔ summary

Sample 2	Grader's Notes
	X no title
Nobody wants air pollution in Joshua Tree National Park. The best solution? Tell the public. Then they can help the problem. Advertisements tell the public about the problem and say what they can do about it.	✓ introduction ✓ begins to state problem and solution ✓ main idea statement X sentence fragment X weak word choices
For example, the Park Service can put ads in newspapers and TV. The ads can tell the problem and ask people to use bus's instead cars. Joshua Tree's dirty air comes from the emissions of millions of vehicles in Los Angeles and San Berdardino. People should ride a bus or train. Their won't be a lot of vehicles and emissions. That means clean air in the citys and clean air in Joshua Tree. Finally, teachers can teach about Joshua Tree in science class.	✓ body X 1 paragraph; needs more development ✓ discusses problem X no details for solution ✓+ uses information from text and new vocabulary X spelling errors/confuses words X last sentence doesn't belong in paragraph
Joshua Tree National Park used to have beautiful, clean air. That's no longer true. People have to know about problems before they can fix them. Ads in the paper and on TV can tell them about the problem and help them start to fix it.	✓ conclusion X repeats, doesn't paraphrase, idea from text ✓ summary of main idea

Sample 3	Grader's Notes
Windmills for Clean Air	✓ title
It's good idea to have clean air in Joshua Tree Park. People with lung sicknes can goes there again. Bad ozone levels in Los Angeles and San Bernardino. Therefore, ozone gets blowed into the park. I think windmills is helping air pollution in Joshua Tree Park.	X no clear introduction, body, or conclusion ✓ main idea ✓ has an unusual solution X verb errors/wrong transition/subject-verb agreement errors/run-on sentence/poor control of verb tenses needs details/examples
Windmills moves the wind in different directions, less pollution drifted over the park. Windmills is making wind power, too. Wind power is helping cities. Through wind power, you clean up the air in Joshua Tree National Park.	✓ spelling and mechanics ✓ summary sentence is simple, but clear

Look at the comparison chart for the three samples. Model your writing after Sample 1.

This writer generally	Sample 1	Sample 2	Sample 3
1. understands the reading	✓	✓	✓
2. responds to the writing prompt	✓		✓
3. paraphrases information and uses new vocabulary from the web page	✓	✓	
4. has an introduction, a body, and a conclusion	✓	✓	
5. writes 4–5 paragraphs; uses correct transitions	✓		
6. writes clear sentences	✓		
7. uses correct grammar	✓	✓	
8. spells and uses mechanics correctly	✓		✓

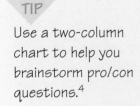
Practice A: Coach Gonzales needs an assistant to help take care of the sports equipment. He puts a job announcement on the bulletin board at school. You want to apply for the job. Write a persuasive business letter in your notebook. Explain to Coach Gonzales why you want the job and why you are the best person for it.

Practice B: Look at the two photographs below. In your notebook, write an expository essay that explores the pros and cons of each job.

SEE PAGE 211 FOR SAMPLE ESSAYS.

Now use your skills to put it all together on Cumulative Practice Test 1.

[4] See page 117 in Chapter 6 to review 2-column charts.

Cumulative Practice Test 1

Mark multiple-choice answers on the Answer Grid on page 192.

Write short answers in this book.
Write paragraphs and longer essays in your notebook.
Use the Checklists on pages 193–194 to review your writing.

Use this reading about comets to answer Questions 1 through 6.

Comets

(1) Comets are great space travelers. (2) It is lumps of ice and dust from the cold outer reaches of the solar system. (3) When it gets close to the sun, the comets ice evaporates. (4) As a result, long jets of gas and dust stream out from the comet. (5) The long jets look like tails.

(6) Long ago, people were afraid of comets. (7) Many written historical documents describe comets causing wars or plagues. (8) Today we know better. (9) In fact, nowadays most people love to look at comets in the night sky while scientists like to study them to learn more about our solar system.

1 **What is the correct way to write sentence 2?**

A Lumps of ice and dust it is from the cold outer reaches of the solar system.

B Their lumps of ice and dust from the cold outer reaches of the solar system.

C They are lumps of ice and dust from the cold outer reaches of the solar system.

D Make no change

2 **In which sentence is all the punctuation correct?**

A When a comet gets close to the sun the comets ice evaporates.

B When a comet gets close to the sun the comet's ice evaporates.

C When a comet gets close to the sun, the comets ice evaporates?

D When a comet gets close to the sun, the comet's ice evaporates.

3 **What is the BEST way to combine these sentences?**

> As a result, long jets of gas and dust stream out from the comet. The long jets look like tails.

A As a result, long jets of gas and dust that look like tails stream out from the comet.

B As a result, long tails stream out from the comet's gas and dust.

C Long jets of resulting streams look like tails.

D Jets of streaming gas-and-dust tails result.

4 **Which sentence could BEST be added after sentence 6?**

A They were afraid of eclipses, too.

B They thought comets were bits of the moon.

C They believed that comets warned of terrible events.

D Even literate people.

5 **Which revision improves sentence 7 by removing the repetition?**

A Many written historical documents describe comets who caused wars or plagues.

B Many historical documents describe comets as the cause of wars or plagues.

C Many written historical records document comets will cause wars or plagues.

D Many written historical war documents record comets that caused plagues.

6 **Look at sentence 9. It is a complex sentence with one independent clause and one dependent clause. Write two simple declarative sentences that express the same ideas as the complex one.**

_____

_____

_____

Read this fable. Then answer Questions 7 through 12.

The Dog and the Shadow

A dog carried a large bone in his mouth. As he (1) _____ across a bridge, he looked down at the water. He (2) _____ his own reflection.

"That dog's bone is (3) _____ than mine," he thought and jumped into the water to get the other dog's bone. He barked (4) _____ he jumped and dropped the bone in his mouth. The water swept his bone down the river. Since there was no other dog and no other bone, the dog was (5) _____ with nothing.

---

7 Which answer should go in blank (1)?

A jog

B joged

C jogged

D joggied

8 Which answer should go in blank (2)?

A saw

B seed

C seen

D seeing

9 Which answer should go in blank (3)?

A big

B bigger

C bigest

D biggest

10 Which answer should go in blank (4)?

A as

B if

C or

D so

11 Which answer should go in blank (5)?

A to leave

B leaved

C leaves

D left

12 Which lesson BEST states the main idea of the paragraph?

A If you grab for shadows, you may lose the substance.

B What is worth the most is often valued the least.

C All that glitters is not gold.

D One good turn deserves another.

Diego's science class is doing research on various foods. Diego is doing his report on potatoes.

13 To complete this assignment, Diego will write _____.

  A a personal narrative

  B a letter to the editor

  C an expository essay

  D a persuasive essay

Before writing his rough draft, Diego organizes his paper by creating an outline. Here is the beginning of his outline:

I. Introduction of topic
II. Early Potato Farming
  A. Incas grew them thousands of years ago
  B. _____

14 What topic belongs under II. B.?

  A Spanish took them home in 16th century

  B Myths about potatoes

  C Plants on space shuttle

  D We eat the root

The following is a draft of one paragraph from Diego's paper. This paragraph may contain errors.

(1) People used potatoes for other things besides eating. (2) The Incas put raw potatoes on breaked bones to make them heal faster. (3) The Spanish learned about potatoes from the Incas around 500 years ago. (4) Some people believed that potatoes cured toothaches. (5) Others wore a slice of baked potato to help their sore throats. (6) Islanders in the south Atlantic Ocean used potatoes instead of money. (7) Miners in Alaska sometimes traded them for gold. (8) The potatoes have vitamin C protecting a miner's bad lung disease.

Strategies for Test-Taking Success: Writing © Heinle, Cengage Learning. Photocopying this page is prohibited by law.

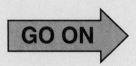

GO ON

15 **What transition word or phrase should be added to the beginning of sentence 1?**

A   As a result,

B   In the past,

C   In the end,

D   For example,

16 **What change, if any, should be made in sentence 2?**

A   change *Incas* to *incas*

B   change *breaked* to *broken*

C   change *heal* to *heel*

D   Make no change

17 **What change, if any, should be made to sentence 6?**

A   change *south* to *South*

B   change *potatoes* to *potatos*

C   change *instead* to *because*

D   Make no change

18 **Which sentence does NOT belong in this paragraph?**

A   Sentence 3

B   Sentence 4

C   Sentence 5

D   Sentence 6

19 **How should sentence 8 be rewritten for precision of word choice?**

A   Vitamin C in the potatoes, which guard against lung disease, is a bad problem for miners.

B   The potatoes protect against a bad vitamin C problem for miners who have lung diseases.

C   The minors use the vitamin C in potatoes to cure lung disease.

D   The vitamin C in potatoes protects against lung disease, a serious problem for miners.

20 **Which sentence matches the tone of Diego's paper?**

A   A lot of stuff the Spaniards got from the Incas was real cool.

B   The Spaniards carried potatoes back to Europe when they sailed for home.

C   The South American culture enlightened their European counterparts with the vast resource this tuber provided.

D   They grabbed everything in sight.

Diego rewrites part of his paragraph. He changes the verb *believed* to an adjective with the ending *–able*.

21 **What is the correct spelling of the new word?**

A believeable

B beliveable

C believable

D beleaveable

22 **If Diego wants to write to his cousin about what he is learning, he should write a _____.**

A letter to the editor

B personal letter

C personal narrative

D business letter

Revise this student information form. Make your capitalization and punctuation corrections on the lines below each item.

Riverside School

23. Date _february 15 2007_

_____

24. Name _alberto v gomez_

_____

25. Address _9614 north mesa street_

_____

26. City/State/Zip _el paso tx 79932_

_____

27. Doctor _dr. Roberto levenson_

_____

GO ON

Write paragraphs and longer essays in your notebook.

Use the Checklists on pages 193–194 to review your writing.

28 **Write a paragraph to answer one of the following questions.**

Topic 1: Text messaging is very popular. But studies show that text messaging may cause writing problems. Why do you think text messaging can cause these problems?

Topic 2: Some people think all music should be free, and they download songs without paying for them. However it is illegal to download music without paying for it. Do you agree or disagree with this law?

---

29 **Writing Task 1**

> The state government has made some budget cuts. As a result, your school will have to cut one program. The school board wants to cut either the music program or the tennis program. Which program do you think your school should keep?
>
> Write a persuasive letter to the school board. Tell the board which program it should keep for your school. Give reasons for your opinion.
>
> Use the Writing Process. Show your work for each step. Use the Checklists on pages 193–194 after you complete each step. Write neatly in your notebook.

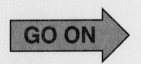

GO ON

The following is an excerpt from a history textbook. It is about the First Amendment of the United States Constitution. Read the excerpt and complete Writing Task 2.

FIRST AMENDMENT FREEDOMS

Freedom of Religion Congress can't pass laws that create state religion. People have the right to worship — or not worship — as they please.

Freedom of Speech Congress can't take away freedom of speech. People living in the United States can agree or disagree with the government. They can say what they think.

Freedom of the Press Congress can't take away freedom of the press. The government can't tell reporters what to write or say in newspapers or magazines, on the radio or on television.

Freedom of Assembly Citizens can meet together peacefully. Citizens have the right to ask the government to change laws.

30   **Writing Task 2**

The First Amendment of the Constitution protects the freedoms of the people who live in the United States. Many countries do not allow their people these freedoms.

Write an essay that explains how the four freedoms in the First Amendment are important to your life.

Use the Writing Process. Show your work for each step. Use the Checklists on pages 193–194 after you complete each step. Write neatly.

STOP. THIS IS THE END OF CUMULATIVE PRACTICE TEST 1.
SEE PAGE 212 FOR ANSWERS AND EXPLANATIONS. STOP

Cumulative Practice Test 2

Mark multiple-choice answers on the Answer Grid on page 192.

Write short answers in this book.
Write paragraphs and longer essays in your notebook.
Use the Checklists on pages 193–194 to review your writing.

Read this story. Then answer Questions 1 through 10.

Gigi Chao and Vincent Perez go to Harbor High School. There are many different clubs activities and teams at the school. But there is no newspaper. So Gigi and Vincent ask Mr. Banker to help them start one. He is their history teacher.

"Students do a lot of things that people don't know about," says Gigi. "For instance, I heard that Jon Friedman won an award for being the best student drummer in the state."

"I didn't know that," says Vincent. "That's great. We can have stories in the newspaper about special things that Harbor students do."

Mr. Banker agrees. He suggests that they write stories about teachers, new classes, and you can even do one about the school building. The art club painted a mural about kids' summer jobs. The mural is in the library.

Gigi is excited. She has another suggestion. She thinks sometimes a student reporter should write the story. Other times, the student or teacher which does something special should write the story.

Vincent adds, "Then a student editor makes sure the stories doesn't have mistakes." He suddenly smiles. "Editor Vincent Perez. Now that sounds good."

"Wait a second," says Gigi. "Editor Gigi Chao sounds better."

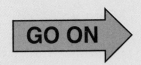
GO ON

Mr. Banker laughs. "You can *both* be editors. You can take turns or share the job. It's a big job, after all."

The next day, the two students put up signs all over the school. They say, "Writers, Photographers, and Cartoonists: Join the new school newspaper! There will be a planning meeting at 4 o'clock in room 18. Come to the meeting after school. Bring your friends. Be prepared for lots of work and lots of fun."

Gigi, Vincent, and Mr. Banker hope nine or ten students attend the meeting. Twenty-five eager students show up. Everyone has a different idea about what stories a school newspaper needs. The cafeteria has new salads. The drama club has a new play. The neighborhood needs volunteers to help clean up the park across the street. The history department has a new course called "Growing Up Global." (Mr. Banker says that this a *very* important story. The students smile.) Everyone wants to be the editor.

There is only one thing they all agree on. Gigi asks, "How does *Harbor News* sound as a name?" Thirty hands go up. (Some kids vote with both hands.)

Mr. Banker smiles and looks around at the students. He looks at the first headline: "Students Start Newspaper. Thanks to History Teacher, Henry Banker."

1 **Which version of this sentence from paragraph 1 shows the correct place to put a comma?**

A There are many different clubs activities and, teams at the school.

B There are many different clubs activities, and teams at the school.

C There are many different clubs, activities, and teams at the school.

D There are many, different clubs, activities, and teams at the school.

2 **How should the underlined part of this sentence be rewritten to create a parallel structure?**

> He suggests they write stories about teachers, classes, and you can even do one about the school building.

A you can even write one about the school building.

B even the school building.

C even write about the school building.

D Leave as is.

GO ON

3 What is the BEST way to combine these statements?

> The art club painted a mural about kids' summer jobs. The mural is in the library.

A The art club, which is in the library, painted a mural about kids' summer jobs.

B The art club painted mural about kids' library jobs in the summer.

C The art club painted a mural in the library about kids' summer jobs.

D The art club, which painted a mural about kids' summer jobs, is in the library.

4 What revision, if any, should be made to this sentence?

> Other times, the student or teacher which does something special should write the story.

A Delete the comma after *time.*

B Change *which* to *who.*

C Insert a comma after *special.*

D Leave as is.

5 What change, if any, is needed in this sentence?

> "Then a student editor makes sure the stories doesn't have mistakes."

A Change *make* to *is making.*

B Change *stories* to *storys.*

C Change *doesn't* to *don't.*

D Leave as is.

6 What revision, if any, is needed in this sentence?

> They say, "Writers, Photographers, and Cartoonists: Join the new school newspaper!"

A Change *They* to *The signs.*

B Delete the comma after *Writers.*

C Change *and* to *or.*

D Leave as is.

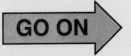
GO ON

7 Which sentence states information already presented and should be deleted from the sign?

A   Join the new school newspaper!

B   Come to the meeting after school.

C   Bring your friends.

D   Be prepared for lots of work and lots of fun.

8 What is the correct way to spell the underlined word?

> The <u>neighborhood</u> needs volunteers to help clean up the park across the street.

A   nayborhood

B   nieghborhood

C   neihgborhood

D   Correct as is

9 How should this sentence be rewritten for precision of word choice?

> He looks at the first headline.

A   He imagines the first headline.

B   He sees the number one headline.

C   He sees the first article title.

D   He imagines the number one article title.

10 Read the two simple sentences below. Combine them into one complex sentence that expresses the same ideas.

> Gigi, Vincent, and Mr. Banker hope nine or ten students attend the meeting. Twenty-five eager students show up.

_____

_____

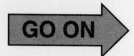

Dear Editor:

I.
     (1) What does our school need most, a bigger auditorium or a bigger gym? (2) There is only enough money in the school budget for one improvement. (3) I'm too young to vote but I'm very involved. (4) The voters' decision affects my classmates and me more than anyone else.

II.
     (5) Years ago, all the students used to fit in the auditorium at one time. (6) Today, the school has to separate the student body in half. (7) That means every performance has to be done twice. (8) Only half of us see some special visitors! (9) The special visitor this year was Senator Brown.

III.
     (10) Everyone also know that our gym is too small. (11) We don't have full-court practices any more because another team is always at the other end of the gym. (12) There also aren't enough seats in the bleachers. (13) Kids stop coming to games when they can't find a place to sit. (14) Teams feel bad when their classmates aren't there to cheer us on.

IV.
     (15) It's easier to make a decision if you think about what goes on in the two places. (16) Most events in the auditorium can move to the gym when there isn't enough room. (17) On the other hand, you can't take a jump shot on the stage, spike a volleyball between the seats, or be stealing the floor-hockey puck down the aisle.

V.
     (18) Someday we may get a bigger auditorium *and* a bigger gym. (19) Until then, please vote in favor of making the gym bigger. (20) That's the smart thing to do for now.

Tamar Alvarez
Green Street School

11 Tamar wants to add this sentence to her first paragraph:

> That's the question the voters will decide next month.

Where should this sentence be added to keep the details in logical order?

A after sentence 1

B after sentence 2

C after sentence 3

D after sentence 4

12 Which version of sentence 3 shows the correct place to put a comma?

A I'm too young, to vote but I'm very involved.

B I'm too young to vote, but I'm very involved.

C I'm too young to vote but, I'm very involved.

D Correct as is

13 How should sentence 6 be rewritten for precision of word choice?

A Today, the school has to take the student body apart.

B Today, the school has to separate the student body into a semicircle.

C Today, the school has to divide the student body in half.

D Today, the school has to disconnect the student body from itself.

14 What is the BEST way to combine these sentences?

> That means every performance has to be done twice. Only half of us see some special visitors!

A That means every performance has to be done twice, only half of us see some special visitors!

B That means every performance has to be done twice, or even worse, only half of us see some special visitors!

C That means every performance has to be done twice; so that only half of us see some special visitors!

D That means every performance has to be done twice, consequently, only half of us see some special visitors!

GO ON

Strategies for Test-Taking Success: Writing © Heinle, Cengage Learning. Photocopying this page is prohibited by law.

15 **What change, if any, is needed in sentence 10?**

A Change *Everyone* to *Everyone's*

B Change *know* to *knows*

C Change *too* to *two*

D Make no change

16 **Which sentence best states the *main idea* of paragraph IV?**

A A bigger gym can hold different activities, but a bigger auditorium can't.

B Making a decision isn't easy.

C You can play music, watch a play, or be listening to a special speaker in the gym or auditorium.

D Your voice isn't heard if you don't vote.

17 **What change, if any, is needed in sentence 14?**

A Change *their* to *there*

B Change *aren't* to *isn't*

C Change *us* to *them*

D Make no change

18 **Choose the answer that is the most effective substitute for the underlined part of the sentence. If no substitute is necessary, choose "Leave as is."**

> On the other hand, you can't take a jump shot on the stage, spike a volleyball between the seats, or be stealing the floor-hockey puck down the aisle.

A take a jump shot on the stage, spiking a volleyball between the seats either, or be stealing the floor-hockey puck down the aisle.

B be taking a jump shot on the stage, spike a volleyball between the seats, or be stealing the floor-hockey puck down the aisle.

C take a jump shot on the stage, spike a volleyball between the seats, or steal the floor-hockey puck down the aisle.

D Leave as is

19 **Which sentence contains a detail that is unimportant to the letter?**

A Sentence 2

B Sentence 9

C Sentence 12

D Sentence 19

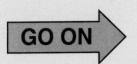
GO ON

The paragraph below is the first draft of Idalia's essay. The draft contains errors. Read the paragraph to answer Questions 20 through 26.

Writing Task: You just won $100. Write a paragraph describing what you would do with the money and why.

A $100 Prize
(1) What would I do with an extra $100? (2) Take my relatives out to dinner.
(3) My relatives is great to me. (4) This special treat is to thank them for everything they do for me. (5) When I came to this country, they buy me clothes and books. (6) Everything I need! (7) My relatives invite me to they're homes all the time. (8) They treat me like a daughter. (9) Why do I need $100?
(10) Were not going to a fancy restaurant. (11) I need $100 therefore I have so many relatives!

20 **What change, if any, is needed in sentence 2?**

   A Insert *I would* at the beginning of the sentence

   B Change *my* to *mine*

   C Replace the period with a question mark

   D Make no change

21 **What change, if any, is needed in sentence 3?**

   A Change *relatives* to *relatives*

   B Change *is* to *are*

   C Change *to* to *two*

   D Make no change

22 **What change, if any, is needed in sentence 5?**

   A Delete the comma

   B Change *buy* to *bought*

   C Insert *to wear* after *clothes*

   D Make no change

23 **How should the underlined word in sentence 7 be written?**

> My relatives invite me to they're homes all the time.

   A they are

   B there

   C their

   D Make no change

GO ON

24 **Which of the following is not a complete sentence?**

A Sentence 1

B Sentence 4

C Sentence 6

D Sentence 9

25 **How should the underlined word in sentence 10 be written?**

<u>Were</u> not going to a fancy restaurant.

A We're

B Where

C Wear

D Make no change

26 **In sentence 11, the word *therefore* does NOT correctly link ideas. Which of these should be used instead?**

A likewise

B still

C consequently

D because

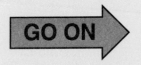

Small Change, Big Savings

Did you know that all your small change adds up quickly? When you fill a big mayonnaise jar to the top with all your quarters, dimes, nickels, and pennies, you will have over $100! Yes, it adds up quickly. If you put that $100 in a savings account, you will earn interest. In this way, your money will earn more money for you. In one year you could have $103. In 10 years, your money will double! How many mayonnaise jars can you fill to the top? Every time you have a full jar, take it to the bank. Start saving now and let your money work for you.

READ THINK EXPLAIN **27** How can a mayonnaise jar help you save money?

_____

_____

_____

READ THINK EXPLAIN **28** Why will putting your money in a savings account help you save money?

_____

_____

_____

READ THINK EXPLAIN **29** What does "let your money work for you" mean?

_____

_____

_____

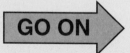

30 **Writing Task 1**

> Several kids at your school were hurt in a car accident. The driver was drunk. You want to start a program to educate teenagers about the effects of drinking and driving. Write a persuasive essay to the student council about the program. Explain why you want to start the program. What will the program do? What do you hope to accomplish?

A. Brainstorm your ideas. Show a 2-column chart *or* a cluster map of your ideas.

B. Organize your ideas into an outline.

Read this passage about an artist named Carlos, his wife, and her friend. Then complete Writing Task 2.

The Luncheon[5]

On the patio, Marta and Rosa set the table for lunch. Marta brushed away the leaves and flower petals. They had fallen from the thick jasmine growing on the trellis around them. Together Marta and Rosa held the corners of the tablecloth. They lifted it in the air, letting it fall gently in place over the edge of the table. Marta smoothed out the tablecloth. Rosa reached for the tray and took the plates, silverware, glasses, and napkins from it.

Carlos looked from behind the easel and canvas he had set up nearby. He watched his wife and her friend as they prepared the table for lunch. The warm sunlight chased the shadows of the jasmine vine. The shadows changed the white of the tablecloth to blue, green, and gray splashed with bright patches of sunlight. Then a fresh breeze moved the leaves. The colors shifted into new shades and shapes.

31 **Writing Task 2**

Write an essay that answers these questions.

What kind of man is Carlos? How can you tell? What is the author trying to tell us about him? Use examples and details from the reading to support your ideas.

Use the Writing Process. Show your work. Use the Checklists on page 187 after you complete each step. Write at least four paragraphs. Write neatly.

STOP. THIS IS THE END OF CUMULATIVE PRACTICE TEST 2.
SEE PAGE 215 FOR ANSWERS AND EXPLANATIONS.

Strategies for Test-Taking Success: Writing © Heinle, Cengage Learning. Photocopying this page is prohibited by law.

[5] Adapted from *Monet, Manet, and Degas Living in Modern Times* by Sophia Wisener with permission from the author.

Strategies for Test-Taking Success: Writing © Heinle, Cengage Learning. Photocopying this page is prohibited by law.

Chapter 8

Get the Best Score

Sun	Mon	Tue	Wed	Thu	Fri	Sat
	1 Today: Make a plan	2 5:00–6 Study time	3 5:00–6 Study time	4 5:00–6 Study time	5 5:00–6 Study time	6 5:00–6 Study time
7	8 5:00–6 Study time	9 5:00–6 Study time	10 Study for science test	11 5:00–6 Study time	12 5:00–6 Study time	13 5:00–6 Study time
14	15 5:00–6 Study time	16 5:00–6 Study time	17 5:00–6 Study time	18 5:00–6 Study time	19 Birthday party for Dad	20 5:00–6 Study time
21	22 5:00–6 Study time	23 5:00–6 Study time	24 5:00–6 Study time	25 5:00–6 Study time	26 5:00–6 Study time	27 School play
28	29 4:00–6 Soccer	30 RELAX	31 TEST			

You have studied the skills you need. You have practiced good test-taking strategies. You have used the Writing Process to answer writing prompts. You are ready for the test. Here are some ideas to get you through test week.

Relax. This is a tense week. Be sure to take time to relax and have some fun.

Be positive about your work. Focus on what you know and what you can do.

Get regular physical exercise. Don't forget to balance schoolwork and exercise. Exercise helps your body be stronger. It helps you sleep well, too, so you can learn better.

On the night before the test:

- **Prepare for test day.** Organize the things you need for the test. Here is a sample list:
  ✓ sharpened pencils and erasers
  ✓ a pen and paper
  ✓ fruit or other healthy snacks for breaks
  ✓ eyeglasses
  ✓ watch
  ✓ a sweater or sweatshirt (in case the room is cold)

- **Eat dinner.** Drink a glass of milk, too. The calcium in milk relaxes you naturally.

- **Relax and don't study.** Studying at the last minute, called cramming, doesn't help. It just makes you worry.

- **Set the alarm.** You don't want to be late for school. Get a good night's sleep.

On the morning of the test:

- **Eat breakfast.** You can't do your best without it!

During the test:

- **Focus on your work.** Don't waste time worrying or wondering how other people are doing. Don't worry about what you did before or what may happen in the future. Pay attention to *what you can do now.*

- **Ask questions.** If you don't understand the directions or if you aren't sure about what you are supposed to do, ask the teacher.

- **Answer the easy questions first.** Then go back and try the hard ones. Don't spend a lot of time on one question. You want to have enough time to finish the whole test.

- **Always make a guess.** Pick the best answer you can. Use the *process of elimination* to help you guess. If you still have blanks, pick one letter and mark any blanks left with that letter.

- **Write neatly.** Make your final copies neat and easy to read.

Good Luck!

Glossary

Adjective part of speech that gives information or details about nouns

Adverb part of speech that gives information or details about verbs, adjectives, or other adverbs

Autobiographical narrative story you write about your own life

Biographical narrative story you write about another person's life

Complete sentence statement with a subject and a verb, a complete thought, and correct end punctuation

Complex sentence independent clause + dependent clause

Compound sentence two independent clauses joined by a comma + *and, but, for, nor, or, so,* or *yet*

Conjunction part of speech that joins words, parts of a sentence, or sentences

Consonant suffix addition to the end of a root that begins with a consonant (*-ful, -less, -ly, -ment*)

Coordinating conjunction one of seven words (*and, but, for, nor, or, so, yet*) used to connect the two independent clauses in a compound sentence

Dependent clause statement with a subject and a verb that does not express a complete thought because it begins with a connector

Exclamation sentence that shows surprise or strong feelings; an exclamation ends with an exclamation point (!)

Expository essay writing of facts about a topic, about how something works, or about why something happened

Homonyms words that sound alike but have different meanings and different spellings

Independent clause statement with a subject and verb that is a complete thought

Interjection part of speech that shows surprise or strong feelings; often followed by an exclamation point (!)

Main idea the most important idea in a reading; also called the *main point* or the *central idea*

Narrative story that can be real or made up

Noun part of speech that names a person, place, thing, or idea

Paragraph unity all the sentences in a paragraph are about the main idea, are in logical order, and no sentences are missing

Part of speech group of words that are alike. English has eight parts of speech: nouns, pronouns, verbs, adjectives, adverbs, prepositions, conjunctions, and interjections.

Persuasive essay writing that tries to change the reader's mind, gives advice, or asks the reader to do something

Preposition part of speech that links a noun or pronoun to another word in a sentence; helps show direction, place, or time

Pronoun part of speech that takes the place of a noun

Proper noun name of a *specific* person, place, thing, or idea; always starts with a capital, or uppercase, letter

Response to literature essay or composition about a work of literature

Root main part or meaning of a word

Run-on sentences sentences that are joined together without correct punctuation or connectors

Sentence fragment incomplete sentence

Simple sentence statement with a subject, a verb, and correct end punctuation; it is a complete thought. A simple sentence is also an *independent clause*.

Standard English language understood by most English speakers

Subject-verb agreement the subject and verb of a sentence match in number (singular or plural) and in person (1st, 2nd, or 3rd)

Suffix addition to the end of a root that changes or adds meaning

Supporting details general information, facts, and examples that support a main idea

Tone how you show what you are thinking or feeling in your writing

Transition change or movement. A transition word indicates the relationship between ideas or paragraphs. Transitions show sequence, time order, comparison, contrast, cause and effect, reasons, conditions, examples, or results.

Verb part of speech that tells what a noun or pronoun *is* or *does*. An *action* verb describes *movement*. A *nonaction* verb describes *feelings* or *how something is*.

Vowel suffix addition to the end of a root that begins with a vowel (*-able, -er, -es, -est, -ed, -ily, -ing*)

Word choice using precise words to say what you mean and avoiding words that are too general or overused

The Writing Process a five-step process that will help you write essays. The five steps are *Plan, Organize, Draft, Revise,* and *Publish.*

Glosario

Adjective (Adjetivo) parte del discurso que proporciona información o detalles sobre sustantivos

Adverb (Adverbio) parte del discurso que proporciona información o detalles sobre verbos, adjetivos u otros adverbios

Autobiographical narrative (Narración autobiográfica) relato que escribes sobre tu propia vida

Biograpical narrative (Narración biográfica) relato que escribes sobre la vida de otra persona

Complete sentence (Oración completa) enunciación con sujeto y verbo que expresa un pensamiento completo y tiene una puntuación final correcta

Complex sentence (Oración compleja) enunciación que consta de una cláusula independiente **más** una dependiente

Compound sentence (Oración compuesta) enunciación que consta de dos cláusulas independientes unidas por una coma **más** una conjunción coordinadora (*and, but, for, nor, or, so, yet*)

Conjunction (Conjunción) parte del discurso que une palabras, partes de una oración u oraciones

Consonant suffix (Sufijo consonante) adición que se coloca al final de una raíz y que empieza con consonante (*-ful, -less, -ly, -ment*)

Coordinating conjunction (Conjunción coordinadora) palabra(s) (*and, but, for, nor, or, so, yet*) que se usa para enlazar dos cláusulas independientes en una oración compuesta

Dependent clause (Cláusula dependiente) enunciación con sujeto y verbo que no expresa *un pensamiento completo* porque comienza con un enlace

Exclamation (Exclamación) oración que expresa sorpresa o sentimientos fuertes; una exclamación termina con un signo de admiración (!)

Expository essay (Ensayo expositivo) composición escrita que refiere hechos sobre algún tema, sobre la manera como funciona algo o sobre las razones por las que algo sucedió

Homonyms (Homónimos) palabras con sonido semejante pero que tienen significados distintos y se escriben diferente

Independent clause (Cláusula independiente) enunciación con sujeto y verbo que expresa un pensamiento completo

Interjection (Interjección) parte del discurso que expresa sorpresa o sentimientos fuertes; va seguida comúnmente de un signo de admiración (!)

Main idea (Idea principal) la idea más importante de una lectura; también llamada *punto principal* o *idea central*

Narrative (Narración) relato; puede ser real o inventado

Noun (Sustantivo) parte del discurso que designa a una persona, un lugar, una cosa o una idea

Paragraph unity (Unidad del párrafo) cualidad del párrafo en el que todas las oraciones giran en torno a la idea principal y siguen un orden lógico, y no faltan oraciones

Part of speech (Parte del discurso) cada uno de los grupos en que se clasifican las palabras según su función. En el inglés hay ocho de estos grupos: sustantivos, pronombres, verbos, adjetivos, adverbios, preposiciones, conjunciones e interjecciones

Persuasive essay (Ensayo persuasivo) composición escrita que busca influir sobre el pensamiento del lector, le da consejos o lo llama a hacer algo determinado

Preposition (Preposición) parte del discurso que enlaza un sujeto o pronombre con otra palabra en una oración; indica dirección, lugar o tiempo

Pronoun (Pronombre) parte del discurso que sustituye al sustantivo

Proper noun (Nombre propio) nombre de una persona, un lugar, una cosa o una idea *específica*; empieza siempre con mayúscula

Response to literatura (Reacción [a la obra literaria]) ensayo o composición escrita sobre una obra literaria

Root (Raíz) la parte principal de una palabra, en la que se encuentra su significado

Run-on sentences (Oraciones seguidas) oraciones que se juntan sin que exista puntuación o enlaces correctos entre ellas

Sentence fragment (Fragmento de oración) oración incompleta

Simple sentence (Oración simple) enunciación con sujeto, verbo y puntuación final correcta; una idea completa. Una oración simple es también una *cláusula independiente*

Standard English (Inglés estándar) lengua entendida por la mayoría de los angloparlantes

Subject-verb agreement (Concordancia sujeto-verbo) el sujeto y el verbo de una oración concuerdan en número (singular o plural) y persona (primera, segunda o tercera)

Suffix (Sufijo) adición que se coloca al final de una raíz y que altera o amplía el significado de ésta

Supporting details (Detalles de soporte) información general, hechos y ejemplos que dan sustento a la idea principal

Tone (Tono) la forma que toma lo que sientes y piensas en tu texto

Transition (Transición) un cambio o movimiento. Una palabra de transición indica la relación entre ideas o párrafos: secuencia, orden temporal, comparación, contraste, causa y efecto, razones, condiciones, ejemplos o resultados, entre otras

Verb (Verbo) parte del discurso que indica lo que un sustantivo o pronombre *es* o *hace*. Un verbo de *acción* describe *movimiento*. Un verbo de *inacción* describe *sentimientos* o *cómo está algo*

Vowel suffix (Sufijo vocal) adición que se coloca al final de una raíz y que empieza con vocal (-*able*, -*er*, -*es*, -*est*, -*ed*, -*ily*, -*ing*)

Word choice (Elección de palabras) el uso de palabras precisas para decir lo que realmente se quiere y la exclusión de palabras demasiado generales o sobreusadas

The Writing Process (El proceso de escribir) proceso de cinco pasos que te ayudará a escribir ensayos. Los cinco pasos son *Planea, Organiza, Haz un borrador, Revisa* y *Publica*

Skills Index

INDEX

INDEX

ANSWER GRID

Print your name in the boxes. Blacken the circle under each letter.

LAST NAME	FIRST NAME	MI

STUDENT ID NUMBER

DIRECTIONS

Use a number 2 pencil

Darken circles completely

Examples:

Wrong

Wrong

Wrong

Right

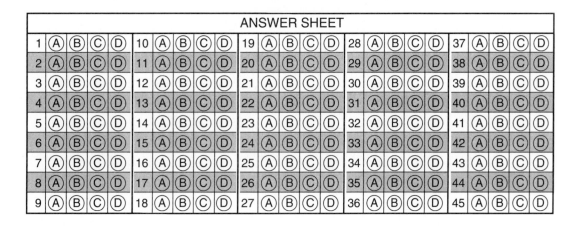

ANSWER SHEET

1	A B C D	10	A B C D	19	A B C D	28	A B C D	37	A B C D
2	A B C D	11	A B C D	20	A B C D	29	A B C D	38	A B C D
3	A B C D	12	A B C D	21	A B C D	30	A B C D	39	A B C D
4	A B C D	13	A B C D	22	A B C D	31	A B C D	40	A B C D
5	A B C D	14	A B C D	23	A B C D	32	A B C D	41	A B C D
6	A B C D	15	A B C D	24	A B C D	33	A B C D	42	A B C D
7	A B C D	16	A B C D	25	A B C D	34	A B C D	43	A B C D
8	A B C D	17	A B C D	26	A B C D	35	A B C D	44	A B C D
9	A B C D	18	A B C D	27	A B C D	36	A B C D	45	A B C D

Organizing Checklist

☑ 1. Are all my ideas about the topic or main idea?
☑ 2. Does the first sentence introduce my main idea?
☑ 3. Are all the sentences in each group about the same idea?
☑ 4. Does the last sentence summarize the main idea?
☑ 5. Did I cross out any ideas that don't belong?

Drafting Checklist

☑ 1. Do I have four to five paragraphs?
☑ 2. Does the first paragraph introduce my main idea?
☑ 3. Does my first sentence get my reader's attention?
☑ 4. Is each paragraph about one supporting detail?
☑ 5. Does the last paragraph summarize the main idea?

Revision Checklist

☑ 1. Is there an introduction, a body, and a conclusion?
☑ 2. Do my subjects and verbs agree?
☑ 3. Are the spelling and punctuation correct?
☑ 4. Can I use better words?
☑ 5. Are my paragraphs in a logical order?
☑ 6. Did I use transitions to connect my ideas?
☑ 7. Can I add information?
☑ 8. Do all the sentences belong?

Revision Checklist for Short Answers

☑ 1. Did I answer the question?
☑ 2. Are my examples clear?
☑ 3. Did I use correct grammar, spelling, and punctuation?
☑ 4. Did I use precise words?
☑ 5. Did I use transitions to connect ideas?

Business Letter Checklist

☑ 1. Is my letter in the correct form?
☑ 2. Does the introduction describe the issue?
☑ 3. Does the body support my opinion?
☑ 4. Does the conclusion summarize the issue and ask for a definite solution?
☑ 5. Is my writing polite?
☑ 6. Is the address correct?

Response to Literature Checklist

☑ 1. Did I read the passage carefully?
☑ 2. Did I read the writing prompt carefully?
☑ 3. Did I organize my essay with an introduction, a body, and a conclusion?
☑ 4. Did I use examples and details from the work of literature to support my main idea?
☑ 5. Is my essay interesting?

Publishing Checklist

☑ 1. Did I include all my revisions and corrections?
☑ 2. Do I have a title?
☑ 3. Did I indent the paragraphs?
☑ 4. Is my handwriting neat and easy to read?

Answer Key

CHAPTER 2
Practices Strategies 3–7
Answers and Explanations

Strategy 3, page 25

Practice A 1. noun: *Rosa* is a person
2. verb: *talk* is the action
3. conjunction: *so* joins two parts of the sentence
4. pronoun: *We* takes the place of Rosa and the speaker
5. adverb: *Once* answers the question *when?*
6. adjective: *lucky* describes the noun *girl*

Strategy 4, page 31

Practice A 1. P: *was seen* is the past perfect tense of *see*
2. R: *is* is the simple present tense of *be*
4. R: *change* is the simple present tense
5. F: *will change* is the simple future tense
Practice B 1. changed 2. took 3. is called
4. allows 5. made 6. showed 7. will be remembered
Practice C Answers will vary. Here is a model.
1. At age five, I lived with my family in Albania.
2. Now I am a student, and I'm learning English fast.
3. In five years, I will be a great writer, and people will love my stories.

Strategy 5, page 34

Practice A 1. S or P: <u>You</u> drive 2. P: <u>states</u> have 3. S: <u>snowmobile</u> makes 4. S: <u>noise</u> scares 5. P: <u>people</u> want
Practice B It ~~were~~ was a place.
So there you ~~has~~ have it. The word ~~come~~ comes all the way from Genoa.

Strategy 6, page 38

Practice A 1. You 2. I 3. They 4. It 5. Its
6. They
Practice B 1. <u>It is</u> in grains, too.
2. <u>They</u> are 15¢ each. 3. They are all good choices for <u>your</u> lunch.

Strategy 7, page 40

Practice A 1. the smallest 2. the best 3. older than 4. the most beautiful 5. more handsome than

---

CHAPTER 2 Review Test
Answers and Explanations, pages 41–43

1. (B) *Verb tenses*
The present tense verb *have* matches the first-person singular subject *I.*

2. (C) *Verb tenses*
The present tense verb *eats* matches the third-person singular subject *he* (Scotty).

3. (C) *Adjectives*
The author is comparing three pets. The *-est* form is correct with the short adjective *cute.*

4. (A) *Adjectives*
The author is describing (not comparing) the parrot, so he needs an *adjective.*

5. (D) *Subject-verb agreement/Pronouns*
The sentence needs a subject. The verb form, *run,* shows that the subject must be plural. *They* is the only plural answer choice.

6. (A) *Noun-pronoun problems*
Every pronoun needs a noun before it. *She* in sentence 1 has no noun.

7. (B) *Pronouns*

Pronouns take the place of nouns. *Your* is a second-person pronoun. *Their* is a third-person pronoun. It matches the plural noun *Women.*

8. (C) *Subject-verb agreement*

The past tense verb *was* matches the third-person singular subject *The prize* (*It*).

9. (C) *Verb tense*

The speaker is talking about an event in the future. So the future tense *will give* is needed.

10. (D) *Verb tense*

The simple past tense of the regular verb *land* is correct. Look at the other verbs in the paragraph. They are in the simple past tense.

11. (A) *Adjectives*

The author is comparing Thaden's time with the time of all the other pilots. The *-est* form is correct with the short adjective *fast.*

12. (A) *Verb tense*

The simple past tense of the irregular verb *come* is correct. All the other verbs in the paragraph are in the simple past tense.

CHAPTER 3
Practices Strategies 8–11
Answers and Explanations

Strategy 8, page 49

Practice A 1. referred For words ending in consonant-vowel-consonant, double the last letter and then add the suffix: re f-e-r (double the *r*) + ed
2. moving For words ending in silent *-e*, take off the *-e* before you add the suffix: move + ing.
3. happier For words ending in a consonant + *y,* change the *-y* to *-i,* then add the suffix: happy happier
4. tomatoes Add *-es* to nouns ending in consonant + *-o.*
Practice B 1. beginning For words that end in consonant-vowel-consonant, double the last letter and then add the suffix.
2. tried For words ending in a consonant and *-y,* change the *-y* to *-i* and then add the suffix.
3. enjoyable No change: For words ending in a vowel and *-y,* add the suffix to the root.
4. happiest For words ending in a consonant and *-y,* change the *-y* to *-i* and then add the suffix.
5. making For words ending in silent *-e,* take off the *-e* before you add the suffix.
6. attachment No change. Suffixes that begin with a consonant do not change the spelling of the root.

Strategy 9, page 52

Practice A 1. to **2.** week **3.** know **4.** weather **5.** It's **6.** Who's **7.** wear **8.** than **9.** Our **10.** past **11.** we're **12.** They're **13.** your

Strategy 10, page 55

Practice A 1. J. K. Rowling (person's initials and name) 3. Jewish (religion) 4. May 17th (month) 5. Native American (ethnic group) 6. Spanish (language) 7. the Great Salt Lake (body of water) 9. Tom (name)

Practice B

Evers High School
1234 Main Street
San Antonio, Texas
(city / state)

Dear Mr. Brand,
(title / name)

    Thank you for the tour of the Witte Museum in San Antonio. Our class is studying animal habitats
    (first word in a sentence / names of organizations)
in Texas Ecology 101. It was exciting to see the different ways that animals live in our state.
    (course names)
    We also loved the H.E.B. Science Treehouse near the San Antonio River.
                       (initials / names of buildings / bodies of water)
    Thank you again for your time and help. We hope to return to the Witte Museum again soon.

Sincerely,
Mrs. Green's Texas Ecology 101 Class
Evers Secondary School

Strategy 11, page 57

End Punctuation

Practice A 1. statement 2. question 3. question
4. statement (Short answers are usually statements.) 5. statement 6. exclamation

Practice B 1. I (statement) 2. C 3. I (question)
4. C 5. I (exclamation) 6. C 7. I (statement)
8. I (statement)

Practice C 1. A blog is a journal or story.
3. Does it cost a lot to have a personal blog?
5. But watch out!
7. You can edit, or change, your blog.
8. Click the "Publish" button to put your blog on the Internet.

Commas, pages 59–60

Practice A 1. the American Falls, the Bridal Veil Falls, and the Horseshoe Falls / series
2. The Niagara River is about 12,000 years old, but the / large number, comma + conjunction
3. June, July, and August / series
4. in winter, so the / comma + conjunction
5. March 29, 1848 / date
6. Until 1912, / introductory words
7. Today, about 12,000,000 tourists / introductory words, large number

Practice B

Before the age of 16, the French boy invented a way for blind people to read and write. introductory words

As a child, Louis Braille was blinded in an accident. introductory words

He went to school, but he only listened. comma + conjunction

The teachers didn't know how to teach him reading, writing, or math. series

Then in 1821, Louis met a soldier named Charles Barbier. introductory words

It used 12 raised dots, and it helped soldiers send messages silently. comma + conjunction

In1829, Louis printed the first Braille book. introductory words

Thanks to a teenage inventor, blind children read, write, and learn any subject they want. series

Apostrophes, Colons, and Semicolons, page 63

Practice A 1. C 2. C 3. His's 4. people's

Practice B

August 26, 200_

To Whom It May Concern:

Tickets for the drama club's production of *The Music Man* will be available on Wednesday, October 12, 2005. There will be performances on Friday, Saturday, and Sunday at 7:30 p.m. Tickets are $5. Come early; seats are limited.

Support drama at your school!

Mr. Minigan
Drama Coach

CHAPTER 3 Review Test
Answers and Explanations, pages 65–67

1. (A) *Spelling/Commonly confused words* The rice belongs to the farmers. Use the possessive pronoun their to show ownership.

 2. (C) *Pronouns*

Pronouns take the place of nouns. He is a third-person singular pronoun. They is a third-person plural pronoun. It matches the plural noun people.

3. (C) *Punctuation/Commas*

Use a comma to separate introductory words from the complete thought.

 4. (B) *Verb tense*

The simple past tense of catch is caught. Other verbs in the paragraph are in the past tense.

5. (D) *Punctuation/End marks*

A. Incorrect. There is no reason to capitalize the common noun *guard*.

B. Incorrect. To add a vowel suffix *(-ed)* to a word ending in a consonant + *y* (cry), change the *y* to *i* and add the suffix. C*ried* is spelled correctly.

C. Incorrect. For most words, the letter combination is *ie*. So *thief* is spelled correctly.

D. *Stop, thief.* It is a command and an exclamation. It is not a question. *Stop, thief* ends in an exclamation point.

6. (C) *Punctuation/Commas*

The two complete thoughts in this sentence are connected with the conjunction *and*. The sentence needs a comma, not a colon.

7. (B) *Punctuation/Apostrophes*
Do not use apostrophes with possessive pronouns.

8. (A) *Punctuation/Commas*
This sentence is made up of two complete thoughts connected with the conjunction but. A comma is needed before the conjunction.

9. (D) *Spelling*
To spell the past tense of *carry*, change the -*y* to -*i*, and add the suffix -*ed*.

10. (B) *Spelling/Commonly confused words*
A. Incorrect. This sentence is made up of two complete thoughts. They are correctly connected with a comma and the conjunction *and*.
B. This sentence needs a verb. The homonym *knew* is the past tense of the irregular verb *know.*
C. Incorrect. The contraction needs an apostrophe to take the place of the *o* in *was not.*
D. Incorrect. This sentence does not show surprise or strong emotion.

11. (C) *Spelling/Commonly confused words*
A. Incorrect. To add a vowel suffix (*–ed*) to a word ending in a consonant + *y* (cry), change the *y* to *i* and add the suffix. *Cried* is spelled correctly.
B. Incorrect. The verb form *leave* is correctly used with the contraction *I'll.*
C. The context of this sentence takes too, which means also.
D. Incorrect. The sentence does not ask a question.

12. October 22, 2005
13. Joseph B. Marcos
14. 9614 North Market Street
15. Tallahassee, FL 32329
16. Washington Street School

CHAPTER 4
Practices Strategies 12–15
Answers and Explanations

Strategy 12, page 72

Practice A
1. C
2. F Sample answer: He doesn't use lighter fluid on the charcoal.
3. F Sample answer: It makes the chicken taste bad.
4. F Sample answer: The grill has to be hot.
5. C
6. F Sample answer: Pink chicken isn't cooked enough.

Practice B Sample answer:
Japan has a flower festival every spring. It is famous all over the world. It is the Cherry Blossom Festival. The flower of the cherry tree is the most popular flower in Japan. It blooms in the spring. People go on picnics and have special parties to see the flowers.

Strategy 13, page 76

Practice A
1. Nine justices, or judges, are on the Supreme Court; furthermore, each justice will serve for the rest of his or her life.
2. The president picks judges for the Supreme Court; however, the Senate can accept or reject the president's choices.
3. The Court gets about 5,000 requests to hear cases each year, yet the justices hear only about 200 of them.
4. Each side sends written statements to the Court; in addition, one lawyer from each side has 30 minutes to speak and answer questions.
5. All nine justices discuss and vote on each case, and a simple majority of five justices decides the case.

Practice A

1. Independent clause: <u>You have to have a car</u>
Dependent clause: (since) <u>you can't walk to a</u>
<u>suburban mall.</u>
2. Dependent clause: (While) <u>there is always a</u>
<u>big parking lot,</u>
Independent clause: <u>there are usually few trees</u>
<u>to shade your car in summer.</u>
3. Independent clause: <u>You will see the same</u>
<u>stores</u>
Dependent clause: (if) <u>you shop in malls across</u>
<u>the country.</u>

Practice B

1. I'm in charge of canned goods and paper
products because I can bend down low to
check out the bottom shelf.
2. Since my sister loves milk and cheese, she is
responsible for dairy products.
3. Mom and Dad decide to cook fish, meat, or
chicken unless we are having an all-vegetable
meal.
4. I didn't want an all-vegetable meal until I
tasted my parents' great vegetarian rice and
pasta dishes.
5. Even though I don't like to shop, our plan
makes it fast and easy.

Strategy 14, page 82

Practice A Sample answers:
1. He works at an auto repair shop that is far
from our home.
2. Mr. Kendal, who owns the shop, trusts my
father with all the cars.
3. My father can fix sedans, sports cars, vans,
and even trucks.
4. My father, who needs to work closer to
home, wants his own shop.
5. He already has a name for the new shop,
which he will call Ng's First-Rate Repairs.

Strategy 15, page 84

Practice A 1. <u>to watch a movie.</u>
Han spends Saturdays emailing friends or
watching a movie.
2. <u>you have to follow the rules of the road.</u>
When you ride your bike, always wear a
helmet and follow the rules of the road.
3. <u>you need to stir</u>
Put cocoa and sugar into the cup, pour in hot
milk, and stir until the milk turns dark brown.
4. <u>they are inexpensive.</u>
Fredo likes Best Boots because they are
comfortable, sturdy, and inexpensive.
5. <u>worked as a reporter.</u>
Mr. Michaels was a soldier, a teacher, and a
reporter.

Practice B

the Arawak, the Carib, and <u>a tribe called the</u>
<u>Ciboney</u> / over 100 islands; and <u>there are 20</u>
<u>countries</u> today / warm and <u>also considered</u>
<u>tropical</u> / to get away from the cold weather, to
lie on the beautiful beaches, and <u>go swimming</u>
around the coral reefs / to snorkel, to fish, and
<u>sailing</u>

Sample revision:

When Christopher Columbus first arrived in
the Caribbean, he found three tribes: the
Arawak, the Carib, and the Ciboney. The
Caribbean includes over 100 islands and 20
countries. The climate in the Caribbean is
warm and tropical. Tourists come in the winter
months to get away from the cold weather, to
lie on the beautiful beaches, and to swim
around the coral reefs. Tourists also like to
snorkel, to fish, and to sail.

CHAPTER 4 Review Test
Answers and Explanations, pages 85–89

1. (C) *Parallel structure*

A. This revision changes the meaning of the sentences by dropping the subject, *He. He,* not his parents, gets them at the bakery and the supermarket or at school.

B. This revision doesn't combine details. In addition, *and I get them at school* is not parallel.

C. This revision correctly makes a compound sentence with parallel structure in the second clause.

D. The semicolons are incorrect. Use semicolons to connect related independent clauses. Also, the connectors *so* and *then* are inappropriate.

2. (A) *Add details*

A. This revision correctly uses *which* to insert a detail about a thing (the name of the recipe).

B. This revision incorrectly uses *who* (only used for people) to insert a detail about a *thing* (the name of the recipe).

C. This revision makes a run-on sentence.

D. The connector *even though* is used to contrast ideas. The ideas in these sentences are similar so even though is incorrect.

3. (B) *Add details*

A and C use inappropriate connectors.

B. This revision correctly combines two details.

D. This revision is a run-on sentence. You can't combine sentences using just a comma.

4. (A) *Sentence types*

A. This revision correctly creates a complex sentence.

B and C are run-on sentences.

D. Independent clauses aren't connected with a semicolon + *and*.

5. (B) *Sentence types*

A. Try out the long form of *you're: Wash* you are *hands* doesn't make sense.

B. You can use a semicolon between two independent clauses with related content.

C. This revision makes parallel details unparallel.

D. This is a run-on sentence.

6. (D) *Sentence types*

A and B are incorrect. *Because they will spread* is a fragment and dependent clause. Semicolons only separate two independent clauses.

C. A comma is missing after *spread*.

D. This revision correctly makes a complex sentence: dependent clause + comma + independent clause.

7. (D) *Sentence fragments*

A. This revision is a run-on sentence.

B. This revision makes a new fragment with *For five minutes*.

C. This revision doesn't fix the fragment. In addition, semicolons only separate two independent clauses.

D. This revision fixes the fragment *For eight to ten minutes*, by connecting it to the independent clause, *Put the cookies in the oven*.

8. (C) *Run-on sentences*

A. The adverb *carefully* is correct. It answers the question, *how?*

B. This revision doesn't correct the run-on sentence.

C. This revision corrects the run-on sentence by separating the two independent clauses with a period. It also starts the new sentence with a capital letter.

D. This sentence is a run-on.

9. Sample answer: I just give them the recipe, so they can make the cookies themselves.

10. (D) *Add details*

A. The connector *however* is used to show contrast, but the details in these sentences are additions.

B and C are incorrect. Those revisions make run-on sentences.

D. This revision correctly uses *who* to insert a detail about a *person*.

11. Sample answer: He wanted the flag to be ready for the new nation. Hopkinson started working early.

12. (A) *Transitions*

A. The connector for this revision has to show contrast between the 13 original stars and the current 50 stars. *Although* shows contrast.

B, C, and D are incorrect. They show cause and effect and conditions instead of contrast.

13. (C) *Parallel structure*

A and B are incorrect. They don't fix the problem with parallel structure.

C. This revision uses the same structure as the first two clauses: color + *for* + meaning.

D. This problem with parallel structure needs to be corrected.

14. Sample answer: Hopkinson represented New Jersey; however, he was born in Pennsylvania.

15. Sample answer: Betsy Ross, an American legend, did not sew the nation's first flag.

16. Sample answer: Hopkinson complained to the government because he wasn't paid for his work.

CHAPTER 5
Practices Strategies 16–21
Answers and Explanations

Strategy 16, page 92

Practice A 1. C 2. B

Practice B Sample answer: Eastern black bears are surprising creatures.

Strategy 17, page 95

Practice A 2, 4

Sample paragraph:

   Native American students planned a science experiment. They compared how potatoes grow in regular soil and man-made soil. The man-made soil was like the red dirt found on Mars. The experiment was nicknamed "Spuds in Space" because NASA picked it for a special ride on the space shuttle.

Practice B

Sample details:

1. You're never lonely with a pet dog. Dogs protect their friends.

2. Educational stations have programs about science, math, and literature. News programs tell you what's going on in the world. There are language courses on some stations.

3. I wanted to be a firefighter when I was a kid. Now, I want to be a computer programmer. I'll take a lot of different courses in college.

Strategy 18, page 99

Practice A 1. I; Hello. What's going on? 2. S 3. S 4. R; Pluto is called a planet, but it may not be one. 5. I; I'll be at your place at 6 o'clock. 6. R; Savings bonds are tax free if you use them for college tuition.

Practice B 1. traveled 2. connected 3. low 4. above 5. higher

Strategy 19, page 102

Practice A 1. From then on (time) 2. In fact, (additional information) 3. Despite (contrast) 4. In contrast to (contrast)

Strategy 20, page 104

Practice A

(4) He never gave up.

(8) Yet the bridge got built

Put sentence 4 after sentence 6.

Put sentence 8 after sentence 5.

Practice B

1. Others say the extra tax is unfair. This sentence is about *opponents* of the bill, while the main idea and all the other sentences are about *supporters* of the bill.

2. ✓ A. This detail is an additional reason why people support the bill.

B is incorrect because it opposes the bill. C is the main idea of a different, contrasting paragraph. (Notice the transition phrase, *In contrast.*)

Strategy 21, page 107

Practice

1. body *But according to* points out that information appeared *before* this section.

2. introduction *My first memories* points out that this is the *beginning* of something.

3. conclusion *In summary* is a phrase that starts a summary.

4. introduction The sentence is about a new study. Because it is about a new study, it is probably at the beginning of an essay.

CHAPTER 5 Review Test
Answers and Explanations, pages 108–113

1. (C) *Paragraph unity*

Ideas A, B, and D are about Corey's first talent show.

C. This idea is about someone else's performance.

2. (A) *Supporting details*

A. This idea is about Corey's first talent show.

B, C, and D are about other places, people, or performances.

3. (D) *Personal narrative*

A, B, and C are incorrect. None of them are about Corey's first talent show.

D. This is the only information about Corey's first talent show.

4. (C) *Transitions*

A, B, and D are incorrect. They are transitions that show additional information, examples, and time order.

C. The transition *However* correctly shows a contrast between loving "cookies and chips" and knowing the author "can't live on junk food alone."

5. (C) *Word choice*

A and B are incorrect synonyms for the context.

C. A scheduled time with a doctor is called a *medical appointment.*

D. This sentence has a problem with precise word choice.

6. (C) *Paragraph unity*

A, B, and D are related details.

C. This sentence is not about the main idea, more healthy foods in school.

7. (D) *Supporting details/Paragraph unity*

A, B, and C have information that is not about healthy foods in school.

D. This sentence logically follows the previous sentences about experiences with the author's parents' medical problems.

8. (B) *Supporting details*

A, C, and D are details about the woodpecker, but they don't expand on the size that is mentioned in sentence 1 (*the largest woodpecker in North America*).

B. This is the only true detail that expands on the statement about the woodpecker's **size**.

9. (C) *Combining sentences*

A and B are run-on sentences.

C. This sentence combines the ideas with a comma + a correct coordinating conjunction.

D. This sentence uses an incorrect transition.

10. (A) *Transitions*

A. The transition *Instead* correctly moves to a contrasting idea.

B, C, and D are incorrect. These transitions show an example, time order, and a result.

11. (D) *Paragraph unity*

A, B, and C are incorrect. These sentences don't link the place the bird was found to the reaction of the birdwatcher in sentence 5.

D. This sentence can be moved because it links the place the bird was found with the reaction of the birdwatcher.

12. (B) *Tone*

A, C, and D are incorrect. All three sentences have the serious tone of the paragraph.

B. The tone of this sentence is too informal. It also uses slang (*Ditto, awesome*), which doesn't fit the paragraph's serious tone.

13. (A) *Supporting details*

A. This sentence provides a useful definition of *rodear*.

B and C are incorrect. Although they give details about Spaniards, those details do not expand on the previous sentence or link it to the next sentence.

D. This detail doesn't belong as a separate sentence here. However, it could be inserted into a later sentence, such as *Cowboys*, also called cowpokes, *led the cattle across open land to a stockyard where they were sold.*

14. (C) *Transitions*

A and B are incorrect. Both phrases have transitions of time order, but they give the wrong time.

C. This transition phrase gives the correct time order.

D. Going to the stockyard isn't the result of the roundup; it follows the roundup. This sentence needs a transition of time order, not cause and effect.

15. (B) *Supporting details*

A, C, and D are incorrect. They all contain details about the history of rodeos, which is the main idea of this paragraph.

B. This sentence is not about the history of rodeos, which is the main idea of this paragraph.

16. (D) *Sentence types*

A. This is a run-on sentence.

B. The connector *however* shows contrast. This sentence needs a connector that shows an additional detail.

C. This sentence is missing a comma between the dependent clause, *When their work was done,* and the independent clause, *the cowboys had time to celebrate,* that follows it.

D. This sentence correctly adds a comma between the dependent clause, *When their work was done,* and the independent clause, *the cowboys had time to celebrate,* that follows it.

17. (B) *Parallel structure*

A, C, and D don't have parallel structure because at least one phrase uses the *-ing* form, and at least one phrase uses the infinitive form, *to* + verb.

B. This sentence corrects the problem by changing the infinitive form, *to brand,* to the *-ing* form so it is parallel with the first two phrases.

18. (D) *Sentence fragments*

A, B, and C are all complete sentences. They have subjects and verbs, form complete thoughts, and use correct punctuation.

D. This sentence is missing a subject and a verb. It is not a complete thought.

19. (A) *Main idea*

A. This sentence is a general statement about all the ideas and details in the paragraph.

B, C, and D are specific details about the main idea, the history of rodeos.

CHAPTER 6
Practices Strategies 22–26
Answers and Explanations

Strategy 22, page 118

Practice A Sample answers:

> The Best Moment in My Life
> trip to Disneyland with my aunt,
> uncle, cousin
> rode a train
> stayed in a motel
> no swimming pool
> saw fireworks

> Beauty is Only Skin Deep
> some people are beautiful, but not good
> good things are inside
> popular
> helpful
> nice hair gets messy

Practice B Sample answers:

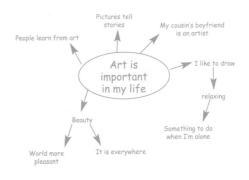

Practice C Sample answers:

Passing a Test to Graduate	
Pros	Cons
1. Everyone learns something.	1. learn how to take the test
2. better education	2. more kids drop out
3. teachers know what to teach	3. only learn what's on the test
4. kids don't graduate and can't read	4. test is hard

Is television harmful?	
Yes	No
1. violence on tv	1. educational stuff on tv
2. some stuff bad for kids	2. gives kids something to do
3. kids get ideas about things that aren't real or true	3. parents control what kids watch
4. bad for eyes	4. bad stuff is on late at night
5. brain isn't working much	5. learn about music and other stuff

page 124
Practice A

I'm Not
~~Im not~~ Shy

    Kids ~~on~~ ^{at} school think I am very shy. I'm ~~quit~~ ^{quiet} and ~~dont~~ ^{don't} talk much. They don't know me too ~~good~~ ^{well}. I talk to the teacher. I say answers when I ~~no~~ ^{know} I'm right. I _{am} not shy ~~an~~ ^{at} home. I talk a lot with my brother. We ~~laughs~~ ^{laugh} and ~~plays~~ ^{play} together. I tell him everything. My brother knows me very well.

He knows I'm not shy.

Strategies for Test-Taking Success: Writing © Heinle, Cengage Learning. Photocopying this page is prohibited by law.

Strategy 24, page 135

Practice A

I am ~~disappoint~~ **disappointed** to read in the ~~newpaper~~ **newspaper** that Bonny Burger will build a ~~resturant~~ **restaurant** on my street. Beulah Guerrero was right to vote against it. It ~~was~~ **will** not be good for the neighborhood.

The ~~resturant~~ **restaurant** will bring more traffic, more ~~noice~~ **noise**, and more pollution. Bayview ~~avenue~~ **Avenue** will never be the same. It will be dangerous for children to cross the street. It will no longer be quiet and peaceful.

It is good that they will add more power and water lines to the area. But this ~~neighborhod~~ **neighborhood** has lots of old houses. Some will ~~tear~~ **be torn** down. This is not good. The new modern building will not fit ~~n~~ **in** and will look ugly.

We ~~dont~~ **don't** need ~~anew resturant~~ **a new restaurant** here. We need the supermarket and ~~job~~ **jobs**. Please ~~to~~ think of a better way to improve our neighborhood than ~~bring~~ **to bring** in a fast-food ~~resturant tht~~ **restaurant that** sells terrible ~~handburgers~~ **hamburgers**.

Strategy 25, page 140

Practice B: Sample revision:

The Main Character in "The Hairy Arm"

Sukeyasu was ~~a~~ **an** independent and brave man. He ~~helps~~ **helped** solve the mystery of the ancient temple.

When he ~~arrive~~ **arrived** in the village, a villager ~~warns~~ **warned** him that the temple ~~is~~ **was** haunted. People ~~which~~ **who** stay there disappear. ~~The villager doesn't like strangers.~~ Sukeyasu is independent. He ~~don't~~ **didn't** pay attention to the ~~villagers~~ **villager's** story. He ~~is~~ **was** cold and afraid, but he ~~stay~~ **stayed** in the temple.

Later he ~~hear~~ **heard** strange noises. Even ~~thought~~ **though** he ~~is~~ **was** worried, he bravely looked in the ~~whole~~ **hole**. When the arm touched him, he ~~doesn't~~ **didn't** yell or ~~running~~ **run** away. He ~~grab~~ **grabbed** the hairy arm and tied it to a chair.

Afterwards, he ~~He~~ went outside. ~~he~~ **He** saw an old badger trying to pull ~~it's~~ **its** arm free. He called the villagers~~,~~ and showed them ~~there~~ **their** ghost. Now they had nothing to be afraid of.

Page 142

Practice Sample outline:

"A Book"

I. This poem is about a boy reading a book
   A. It changes him
   B. It makes his life better
II. What he was like before reading the book
   A. He was poor
   B. He was quiet and sad
   C. He didn't have much hope
III. What he was like after reading the book
   A. His spirit felt strong
   B. He forgot his troubles
   C. He had hope
IV. The boy was changed after reading the book.
   A. It gave him hope
   B. It made his life better

Sample response to literature:

"A Book"

The poem "A Book" describes how a poor boy changes after he reads a story. It fills his spirit and gives him hope. It helps make his life better.

Before reading the book, the boy seems hungry, maybe for food or happiness. He is poor and sad. His days are gloomy. He doesn't have much hope for the future.

After he reads the book, he is happier. The words fill his spirit like food fills a belly. The book lets his mind fly away from his situation, so he forgets about his troubles. He sees new chances, and that gives him hope.

The boy changes after reading the book. Before, he feels sad and hopeless. The story makes him forget his troubles and gives him hope. It makes him feel better about life.

Strategy 26, page 145

Practice A

The History of Kentucky

Have you ever been to Kentucky. [?] Kentucky is one of the ~~oldes~~ [oldest] territories in the United ~~states~~. [States]
It has a long history, and many famous people lived there. ~~Its~~ [It's] rich with traditions, such as horse racing.

Kentucky ~~is~~ [was] first part of ~~virginia~~ [Virginia]. In 1792, it ~~become~~ [became] the 15th state to join the ~~union~~. [Union] Settlers
~~went there starting~~ [started going there] around [the] 1770s. Later, Kentucky played an important role in the Civil War
and the ~~underground railroad~~. [Underground Railroad]

Lots of famous people lived in Kentucky. Abraham Lincoln was born there. ~~Hs~~ [His] wife, Mary Todd,
lived in Lexington until she married. Stephen Foster wrote "My Old Kentucky Home" while
visiting his cousin.

Now Kentucky is most famous for a horse race called the Kentucky Derby. Kentucky is [called]
the ~~Bluesgrass state~~ [Bluegrass State,] because of the limestone in the ground. It makes the grass look blue. It is
good for the ~~horse~~ [horses,] who get strong from eating the bluegrass.

Kentucky is a very interesting state. It has a long, rich history. It was the home of many
historic Americans. And the bluegrass is ~~beutiful~~. [beautiful] Please come visit.

Answers and Explanations, pages 147–149

1.

How to Whistle

Do you know how to whistle_^<del>.</del> **?** If you <del>dont</del> **don't**, here are three easy steps to follow. Practice them<del>.</del> _^**, and**

I promise you will be whistling in no time.

_____First, make a tiny circle with your lips<del>.</del> **, just** <del>Just</del> big enough for air <del>can</del> pass **to** <del>threw</del> **through. Second** <del>Next,</del> put the

tip of your tongue behind your bottom teeth. Third, blow out air through your mouth. Try not to

blow <del>to</del> **too** hard. <del>Its</del> **It's** easier to whistle with a small amount of air. To make your first note<del>.</del> _^**, you** <del>You</del> may

have to move your tongue or change the circle formed by your lips.

Now that <del>Since</del> you can make a sound, it's time to experiment. Change the strength of your breath to

produce <del>other</del> **another** _^ note. Above all, practice. <del>You</del> **Soon, you** will be <del>whistle</del> **whistling** _^ your favorite songs.

2. Sample answers:

Plan Brainstorm and write down all your ideas about the topic.

Organize Put your ideas in order. Use a graphic organizer or write an outline.

Draft Write your ideas in paragraphs. Use your graphic organizer or outline as a guide.

Revise Reread your draft and correct all the mistakes.

Publish Write your essay again with no errors. Write neatly because this is what the grader reads.

 3. (C) *Capitalization*

A. The sentence needs a subject and verb, so the contraction of *It is* is correct.

B. The word *the* would only be needed if the doctor's name didn't follow his title.

C. Titles are capitalized when they are followed by names.

D. The title, *dr.,* needs to be capitalized.

4. (C) *Transitions*

A and B are incorrect. These transitions mean *before*. The new rule is for the future.

C. This is the only transition that links the rule with its result.

D. This transition means during the voting, which is in the past. The new rule is for the future.

5. (A) *Parallel structure*

A. This revision corrects the clause that is inserted into a series of three nouns.

B. This revision doesn't correct the problem in parallel structure; it only moves the unneeded clause in the noun series.

C. This revision removes the commas that are needed to separate items in a series, and the problem with parallel structure is not corrected.

D. This problem with parallel structure needs to be corrected.

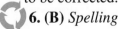 **6. (B)** *Spelling*

A, C, and D are incorrect.

B. This is the correct spelling because it follows the rule of *i before e.*

7. (B) *Sentence combining*

A. This revision is a run-on sentence.

B. This is the only answer that correctly inserts information without changing meaning.

C. This changes the meaning; Marta Gonzales was not the only board member to vote.

D. The connector *however* shows contrast, but the two clauses mean the same thing.

8. *The Writing Process/Persuasive letter*

Sample Plan

Baning Soft Drinks

ban is a good idea

sugar is not good for health

bad for teeth

~~went to the dentist twice this year~~

some people think kids should make
   their own decisions

kids will eat & drink what they like
   more than what's good for them

more than water, milk and juice

greentea

Sample Outline

I. Support your decision.
   A. Thank you for banning soft drinks
   B. Sugar is bad for health and teeth
II. Some people think kids can make own decisions
   A. Kids are old enough, but still don't
   B. They pick what they like, not what's healthy
III. One suggestion
   A. Water, milk, juice are boring; we need more choices
   B. green tea, hot chocolate

March 15, 2007`
Cane Bay School Board
3540 School Road
Cane City, AK 60405

Dear Members of the Board,

Thank you for ~~baning~~ banning soft drinks in the Cane ~~bay~~ Bay schools. ~~To~~ Too much sugar is not very healthy.

Some kids think they can ~~deside~~ decide on ~~they're~~ their own. But ~~Im~~ I'm a teenager, and I can tell you that most kids choose what they like, not what is ~~health~~ healthy . If they ~~didnt~~ didn't, we wouldn't need to have the band.

I do have one suggestion. Water, milk, and juice are okay, ~~so~~ but what about green tea and hot chocolate? This will give us more ~~choice~~ choices; without soft drinks.

Sincerely,
~~Sincerly~~
Mia Yan

CHAPTER 7
Practices Strategies 27–28
Answers and Explanations

Strategy 27, pages 155–156

Practice A Sample answers:

Topic 1: Watching TV Can Be Useful

It is true that you can waste time watching TV; however, you can also learn things from TV. For example, some college courses are on television. You can watch TV to earn college credits. In addition, there are programs for news, government, and the arts. They are educational and a good use of your time.

Topic 2: CD-ROM vs. DVD

CD-ROMs and DVDs look alike, but they do different things. They are the same size and shape, although a DVD holds more data. A CD-ROM can play music, while a DVD can play a movie. These are the main differences between CD-ROMs and DVDs.

Practice D
Using Exaggeration

Exaggeration makes a story more exciting. A fisherman wants to share the most exciting part of his tale, not the ordinary part. He thinks people won't listen to the simple truth. For a storyteller, telling a good story is more important than telling the truth.

Practice E
Sample Paragraph:

Siginate comes from seaweed. When it is put in foods, it makes them much healthier. It doesn't have any taste or smell, so it can be added to people's favorite foods. It can also help people lose weight. They won't want to eat too much after eating food with siginate.

Strategy 28, page 162

Practice A

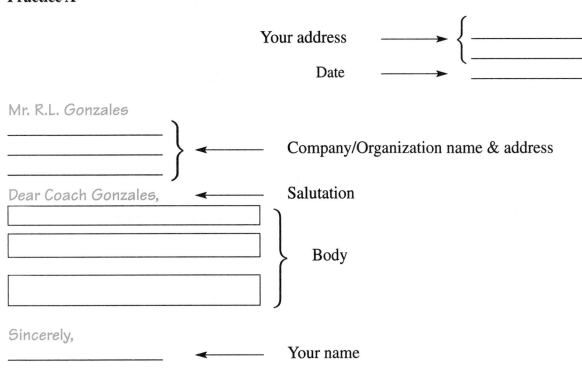

Practice B
Sample 1. Very Good Score

Office Worker or Pilot?

How do you decide whether to work in an office or to fly a jet? Both have good and not so good things about them. It depends on what kind of person you are.

Working in an office is steady, regular work. You get to work inside, talk to many people, and use computers. This is fine for a lot of people. Other people think its boring. They want to work outside. In addition, some people don't like talking to people on the telephone all day long.

Many people think flying a jet is very exciting. It's an adventure because you get to travel to far away places. But it is dangerous work. Some people don't like to fly, or they are afraid of heights. This would not be the best job for them.

In conclusion, both jobs have good things about them. But whether you would pick one job or the other depends on what you like to do. For people who want a steady job, working inside, and talking to people, the office is for you. However, if you like danger, adventure, and flying high, learn to be a pilot.

Sample 2. Poor Score

Its boring working in a office. Its excite to fly a jet. I would like fly a jet better then working in a office It would be more exciting. It be like being on an really cool advensure every day.

If I can pick my favorite job either working in an office or fling a airplane I would pick the airplane. It would be more fun.

Sample 1 responds to the writing prompt, has all the parts of a good essay, writes clear sentences, and uses transitions. Grammar, spelling and mechanics are strong.

Sample 2 responds to the writing prompt, but is missing many parts of a good essay. The writer repeats, but does not develop ideas. Spelling and mechanics are weak.

CHAPTER 7 Cumulative Practice Test 1
Answers and Explanations, pages 163–170

1. (C) *Pronoun reference*

A and D are incorrect because they use the singular *it is* to refer to the plural noun *comets* in sentence 1.

B. *They are* is confused with the possessive pronoun *Their.*

C. The plural *They* are refers to the comets in sentence 1.

2. (D) *Punctuation/Apostrophes, commas*

A and B are missing the comma between a dependent and an independent clause. The apostrophe in the possessive of *comets* is also missing in A.

C. Incorrect. A statement does not end with a question mark.

D. A comma separates a dependent clause from an independent clause. An apostrophe in the possessive of *comets* is correct.

3. (A) *Combining sentences*

A. This revision correctly inserts a detail into another sentence.

B, C, and D change the meaning of the sentences.

4. (C) *Paragraph unity*

A and B are incorrect because they are unrelated details.

C. This sentence best links sentences 6 and 7.

D. This is a sentence fragment.

5. (B) *Word choice/Repetition*

A, C, and D are incorrect because they do not remove the repeated words, *written, records,* and/or *documents.*

B. This revision correctly removes the repeated words, *written* and *documents.*

6. Sample short answer: In fact, nowadays most people love to look at comets in the night sky. Scientists like to study them to learn more about our solar system.

7. (C) *Spelling/Suffixes*

C. For words ending in consonant + vowel + consonant, double the last consonant, and then add the suffix; so *jog* + *ed* becomes *jogged.*

8. (A) *Verb forms/Irregular verbs*

A. The other verbs in the paragraph are all in the simple past tense. The simple past tense of the irregular verb *see* is *saw*.

9. (B) *Adjectives*

B. The dog is comparing two bones. The *-er* form is correct. For words ending in consonant + vowel + consonant, double the last consonant, and then add the suffix; so *big + er* becomes *bigger*.

10. (A) *Transitions*

A. The transition *as* correctly links two things happen at the same time: *barking* and *jumping*.

B, C, and D are incorrect. These transitions show conditions, choices, and cause and effect.

11. (D) *Verb forms/Irregular verbs*

D. The past participle of leave is *left*.

12. (A) *Main idea*

A. This moral is the best summary of the main point of the fable.

13. (C) *Kind of writing*

A. A personal narrative is a story about an event in someone's life.

B. A letter to the editor is a persuasive essay that supports one side of an issue.

C. An expository essay is a researched report on a topic.

D. A persuasive essay examines one or more sides of an issue.

14. (A) *Outlining*

A. II.B. is about the history of potato farming. This is the only answer choice that mentions history.

15. (B) *Introductory phrases*

A, C, and D are incorrect. They are phrases that introduce paragraphs about cause and effect, a summary, and an example.

B. The phrase *In the past* correctly sets the context and introduces the paragraph.

16. (B) *Verb forms/Irregular verbs*

B. The past participle of *break* is *broken*.

17. (A) *Capitalization*

A. Capitalize the first letter of each word in the name of a body of water, including words that are sometimes directions.

18. (A) *Paragraph unity*

A. The main idea of this paragraph is "In the past, people used potatoes for other things besides eating." Sentence 3 is a detail about the history of potatoes.

19. (D) *Word choice*

D. This is the only sentence that correctly states that a vitamin in potatoes protects (not guards or cures) against lung disease, which is a problem for miners (not minors).

20. (B) *Tone*

A. Standard English does not use slang (*stuff, real cool*).

B. This sentence has good, clear ideas and uses standard English, good grammar, and correct spelling and capitalization.

C. This sentence uses extremely academic language that doesn't fit the tone of the paragraph.

D. Standard English does not use slang (*grabbed everything in sight*).

21. (C) *Spelling/Suffixes*

C. For words ending in a silent *-e (believe)*, drop the silent *-e* before adding a suffix starting with a vowel.

22. (B) *Kind of writing*

B. Write a personal letter to friends or relatives.

23. February 15, 2007

24. Alberto V. Gomez

25. 9614 North Mesa Street

26. El Paso, TX 79932

27. Dr. Roberto Levenson

28. Sample answers:

Topic 1

There are several problems with text messaging. First, it uses language shortcuts. These shortcuts can be confusing. Second, some kids think text messaging is the way words are really spelled. Then they learn poor English. Third, it can be very expensive. Besides, it is more fun to talk than to text.

Topic 2

Downloading music for free is illegal for good reasons. Musicians work hard to make good albums. They have a right to earn a living. Music companies spend a lot of money to make and sell albums, too. Maybe a few musicians and companies make too much money. But most musicians don't. Kids get upset when they don't get paid for their work. So it's only fair that they pay when they download other people's work.

29. Sample plan:

Please Keep Our Music Program	
Music	Tennis
1. More kids play music	1. Only a few kids play tennis
2. Music helps kids learn math	2. They can play in the park
3. School band plays at football games	3. ~~I like basketball better~~
4. Students can get instruments	4. Tennis rackets are not so expensive
5. Only place to learn music	

Sample draft of the body:

Another reason to keep the music program is that band is the only place some kids can learn music. You can go to the park for tennis. You need a place like school to lern music instruments are expensive to buy. The school can give them the instruments to learn how to play. Without no school music program, many kids never play music.

30. Sample outline:

The First Amendment's Four Freedoms
I. The 4 freedoms let me live the way I want.
  A. Religion, Speech, Press and Assembly
    1. Lets me decide how to live.
    2. I can say what I want about the govt.
II. Freedom of Religion and Speech
  A. Pray in different ways
    1. My friends and neighbors can go to mosques, temples, or churches.
  B. You can talk about the government if you don't like something about it.
    1. My dad was upset about gas taxes.
    2. He can talk about it and not be afraid.
III. Freedom of the Press and Assembly
  A. I can read or listen to anything I want.
    1. Write about when people in the government do something wrong
    2. Makes the government do the right thing.
  B. If people don't like something the government does, they can get together.
    1. A lot of people can show the government what they think.
IV. The country stays free because we have four freedoms.

Sample draft of the introduction:

The First Amendment's Four Freedoms

The First Amendment freedoms are the most important parts of the U.S. Constitution. They are the Freedom of Religion, Speech, Press, and Assembly. These freedoms let me decide how I want to live. These freedoms also let me say what I think about the government.

CHAPTER 7 Cumulative Practice Test 2
Answers and Explanations, pages 172–182

1. (C) *Punctuation/Commas*

C. Commas separate items in a series of three or more: *clubs, activities, and teams.*

2. (B) *Parallel structure*

A and C are incorrect. They don't fix the problem with parallel structure.

B. This revision has the structure most similar to the first two nouns in the list.

D. This problem with parallel structure needs to be corrected.

3. (C) *Combining sentences*

A, B, and D are incorrect. Each one changes the meaning of the sentences.

C. This revision combines the sentences and removes the repeated word *mural.*

4. (B) *Adding details*

A. This comma is needed to separate the introductory phrase from the sentence.

B. Use *who* to insert a detail about a person: the student or teacher.

C. There is no reason to insert a comma.

D. This problem with *which* needs to be corrected.

5. (C) *Subject-verb agreement*

A. The other sentences in the paragraph are in the simple present tense.

B. The plural of *story* is correct *(stories).*

C. The plural stories takes a plural verb, *don't (do + not).*

D. The plural *stories* needs a plural verb, *don't (do + not).*

6. (A) *Pronoun reference*

A. It is unclear if *They* refers to the two *students* or the *signs.*

B. The comma is needed to separate a direct quotation from the rest of the sentence.

C. The coordinating conjunction *and* correctly adds details.

D. The pronoun reference isn't clear.

7. (B) *Unnecessary repetition*

A, C, and D all give new information.

B. The previous sentence states that there will be a planning session at 4 o'clock. *Session/meeting* and *4 o'clock/afternoon* repeat the same information.

8. (D) *Spelling*

A, B, and C are incorrect.

D. This is the correct spelling. It follows the rule of *-e* before *-i* when pronounced as *-ay.*

9. (A) *Word choice*

A. This revision uses the word *imagines* precisely instead of *sees* and keeps the other correct word choices.

B, C, and D misuse the words *see* (for *imagines*), *number one* (for *first*), and/or *title* (for *headline*).

10. Sample sentence: Gigi, Vincent, and Mr. Banker hope nine or ten students will attend the meeting; instead, 25 eager students show up.

11. (A) *Adding details*

A. This sentence logically responds to the question that introduces the letter.

12. (B) *Punctuation*

A, C, and D need commas before the coordinating conjunction *but.*

B. This sentence combines the ideas with a comma + the correct coordinating conjunction.

13. (C) *Word choice*

A. *To take something apart* means to break it into pieces. It doesn't mean *half.*

B. A *semicircle* is a shape, not an amount.

C. You *divide* a number in half. This is the best word choice.

D. You *disconnect* an object; you can't disconnect a group from itself.

14. (B) *Sentence combining*

A. This is a run-on sentence.

B. This sentence correctly combines the two complete thoughts with a comma + the coordinating conjunction *or* + connectors *even worse.*

C. The second clause in this answer is a dependent clause, but semicolons only connect two independent clauses.

D. This answer is incorrect. A complex sentence connected by *consequently* needs a semicolon, not a comma.

15. (B) *Subject-verb agreement*

A. *Everyone's* means *Everyone is,* which doesn't make sense.

B. The singular subject *Everyone* takes the singular verb *knows.*

C. In this sentence, *too* means very, not the number 2.

D. The subject *Everyone* and the verb *know* don't agree.

16. (A) *Main idea*

A. This states the general idea of the paragraph.

B. This is a detail.

C. This sentence states the main idea and doesn't have parallel structure.

D. This sentence doesn't belong in this paragraph.

17. (C) *Noun-pronoun problems*

A. The possessive pronoun *their* is correct.

B. The plural noun *classmates* takes the plural verb *aren't.*

C. Pronouns take the place of specific nouns. This pronoun refers to the third- person plural *Teams.* The pronoun also needs to be third person plural—*them.*

D. This sentence has a noun-pronoun problem.

18. (C) *Parallel structure*

A, B, and D don't have parallel structure.

C. This revision correctly makes all three phrases parallel in structure: *a verb + a noun + a prepositional phrase.*

19. (B) *Paragraph unity*

A, B, and D are supporting details.

B. The name of a speaker is a detail that doesn't support the main idea of the letter.

20. (A) *Sentence fragment*

A. This is a sentence fragment that is missing both a subject and a verb.

B. There is no problem with the possessive pronoun *my.*

C. This is a statement, not a question, so a period is the correct end punctuation.

D. This is a sentence fragment.

21. (B) *Subject-verb agreement*

A. This synonym is not a precise word choice.

B. The plural *relatives* takes the plural verb *are.*

C. The context of this sentence takes the preposition *to.*

D. This sentence has a problem with subject-verb agreement.

22. (B) *Verb tense/Irregular verbs*

A. The comma is needed to separate the dependent clause from the independent clause.

B. The sentence context is in the past, and the other verb in the sentence is in the simple past tense. The simple past tense of the verb *buy* is *bought.*

C. Adding *to wear* would make a problem with parallel structure.

D. There is a problem with verb tense.

23. (C) *Commonly confused words*

A. The sentence doesn't make sense if you substitute *they are* for *they're.*

B. This sentence needs the possessive pronoun *their,* not an adverb that shows place.

C. The plural possessive pronoun *their* correctly modifies *homes.*

D. The sentence doesn't make sense if you try to substitute *they are* for *they're.*

24. (C) *Sentence fragment*

C. *Everything I need!* is not a complete thought. It needs a subject and a verb.

25. (A) *Commonly confused words*

A. Use the contraction *We're* to provide a subject and verb in this sentence.

B. This sentence needs a subject and verb, not an adverb that shows place.

C. *Wear* means *to put on clothing.*

D. This sentence is missing a subject.

26. (D) *Transitions*

A, B, and C are transitions that show similarity, contrast, and results.

D. The transition *because* correctly shows a cause and effect relationship.

27. Sample answer: It's easy to put a little change in a mayonnaise jar every day. When it is full, you will have over $100. If you fill many mayonnaise jars, you can save hundreds of dollars.

28. Sample answer: A savings account can help you save money because the bank pays you to keep your money there. This is called interest. The interest is added to the money you put in, so you have more money than when you started.

29. Sample answer: "Let your money work for you" means your money can earn money. If you put $100 in a jar, it stays $100. But if it earns interest, you get more than $100. That's how it "works" for you.

30. A Sample two-column organizer:

A "Stop Drinking and Driving Program"	
What	Start a new program to stop drinking and driving
Why	1. Friends hurt by a drunk driver 2. Information about the dangers 3. Learn how to stop it
How	1. Invite a police officer to talk about it 2. Write a play about drinking and driving 3. Make posters 4. ~~Learner's permit classes~~ 5. Talk about designated drivers
Who	The student council
Goal	1. To stop drinking and driving 2. Make the town safer 3. Save lives

B. Sample outline:

A New "Stop Drinking and Driving" Program
I. Drunk driver hurt our friends
  A. People need to know about the risk.
    1. What can happen
    2. How to stop it
  B. We can reach out to people about it.
II. What we can do to teach people
  A. Get people to talk about drinking and driving
    1. Invite speakers
    2. Put on a play
    3. Show a movie
  B. Make posters
    1. Information
    2. Reminders
  C. Talk about a designated driver program
III. The goal: stop drinking and driving
  A. This will reduce the number of accidents
    1. Make everyone safer
  B. It will save lives
IV. Get the student council to help
  A. Explain the risks of drinking and driving
  B. It will make the town safer
  C. It will save lives

31. Sample cluster map:

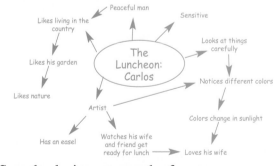

Sample closing paragraph of essay:

Carlos is a sensitive man. He is quiet and peaceful, and he loves nature. He looks at things very closely. He notices how light and movement change colors. He looks at the world like an artist. Maybe he is a very good artist.